the BATTLE of FRANKLIN

The Battle of Franklin

Twilight of the Army of Tennessee

James A. Crutchfield

Providence House Publishers
WWW.PROVIDENCEHOUSE.COM
FRANKLIN, TENNESSEE

TENNESSEE HERITAGE LIBRARY

Printed in the United States of America

13 12 11 10 09 1 2 3 4 5

Library of Congress Control Number: 2009938232

ISBN: 978-1-57736-438-2

Cover design by LeAnna Massingille

Inset cover photo by Mary Lawson
Historic cover photos courtesy of Rick Warwick

Chapter opener illustration from Franklin: A Photographic Recollection Vol. 1, *copyright 1989 by Bob and Jackie Canaday*

This volume is an excerpt from the book Franklin: Tennessee's Handsomest Town

PROVIDENCE HOUSE PUBLISHERS
A Hillsboro Press book
238 Seaboard Lane • Franklin, Tennessee 37067
800-321-5692
www.providencehouse.com

CONTENTS

Franklin and the War Between the States: 1861–1863 1

The Battle of Franklin: 1864 19

The Aftermath of the Battle of Franklin: 1864–1865 43

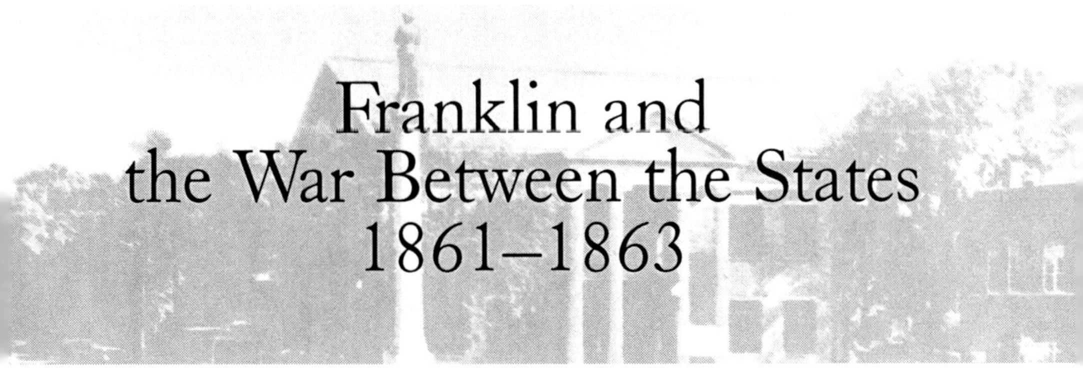

Franklin and the War Between the States 1861–1863

ON DECEMBER 20, 1860, in a specially called state convention at Columbia, South Carolina, delegates passed an ordinance which dissolved the union between that state and the rest of the nation. A few days later members of the convention requested that the Federal government surrender the Charleston Arsenal, along with Forts Moultrie and Sumter and Castle Pinckney. As the end of the year approached and no response from Washington was received, South Carolina troops moved to occupy Moultrie and Pinckney and to seize the arsenal in Charleston.

The month of January 1861, opened and closed with a rapid succession of takeovers by Southern states of Federal properties within their boundaries, following the precedent of South Carolina the month before. The occupation by Southern troops of United States' military installations on Southern soil continued until virtually all shore forts and Federal arsenals in the South were in the hands of the Confederate government.

The name of Fort Sumter, however, a strong fortress guarding Charleston, was noticeably absent from the list of occupied properties. On April 12, 1861, Confederate batteries on the mainland, commanded by General P. G. T. Beauregard, opened fire on Fort Sumter. The installation's 128 defenders resisted bravely, but the four thousand Southern troops they faced were simply too strong. At 2:30 P.M. on April 13, a defeated, but still proud, Union garrison surrendered. The falling of Fort Sumter to Confederate troops that spring day heralded the beginning of the War Between the States.

ABOVE
In mid-April 1861, residents of Franklin, like those in all other Southern towns and cities, were rather taken aback when they learned that elements of the Southern army had occupied Fort Sumter in Charleston Bay. Within one month after the event, young men and boys from Franklin had organized their first unit to serve with the Confederate States of America. (Drawing from Harper's Pictorial History of the Civil War*)*

One by one, Southern states seceded from the Union and joined the newly formed Confederate States of America. Tennessee was the last state to cast its fate with the Confederacy, doing so in June 1861. The secession question had been put to popular vote and 105,000 residents of the state voted to secede while only forty-seven thousand voted to remain in the Union. Most of the secessionist votes came from Middle and West Tennessee, regions which both lent themselves to a plantation and slave-holding economy. Conversely, the vast majority of residents in mountainous East Tennessee, an area comprised of small, family-owned farms, voted overwhelmingly to remain in the Union.

Residents of Franklin lost little time in demonstrating their support for the Southern cause. Soon after the first shots were fired at Fort Sumter, Company D of the First Tennessee Infantry Regiment was recruited from fighting-age men in the vicinity. In the presence of the unit's officer corps, consisting of Captain James P. Hanner, First Lieutenant John L. House, Second Lieutenant William G. Marshall, and Third Lieutenant Carey A. Harris, the men of Company D were mustered into service in Franklin on May 9. The nine-year-old girl who as an adult became Mrs. Newton Cannon left a vivid description of the men of Company D preparing to leave Franklin for training at Camp Cheatham in Robertson County. She wrote:

> The 18th of May, 1861, was the day set for the Williamson Greys [*sic*] (as they were called) to depart . . . to be drilled for actual service, a never-to-be-forgotten day for the mothers, sweethearts, and friends. Early in the day the Company was drawn up in front of the Presbyterian Church. After a prayer by our Presbyterian pastor, soldiers were presented with a pocket testament. The thoughtless fellows . . . threw them in the mud puddles by the side of the road on their way to the station; others carried them through the war, and one was sent back from Atlanta, stained with the lifeblood of our young relative. . . .

On May 28, two additional companies—one infantry and one cavalry—of Franklinites and their neighbors were mustered into Southern service: Company H, Twentieth Tennessee Infantry Regiment (the "Marion Rifles"), led by Captain Moscow Carter, First Lieutenant M. Fountain Degraffenreid, Second Lieutenant Richard Swanson, and Third Lieutenant Philomon H. Eelbeck; and Company C, First Tennessee Cavalry Battalion (the "Williamson County Light Dragoons"), commanded by Captain William Ewing, First Lieutenant Burke Bond, Second Lieutenant Isaac S. House, and Third Lieutenant Joseph B. S. Wyatt.

Autumn of 1861 witnessed additional company organizations in Franklin. On September 28, at Carnton, the home of John McGavock, Company F, Eighth Tennessee Cavalry Battalion (the "Williamson County Cavalry") was raised with Captain James W. Starnes commanding. Other officers were First Lieutenant William S. McLemore, Second Lieutenant Thomas F. P. Allison, and Third Lieutenant T. L. Green Harrison. Two weeks after the formation of

Company F, the *Western Weekly Review,* Franklin's newspaper, proudly proclaimed that:

> Another fine cavalry company was organized at this place last Saturday and mustered into the service. . . . It numbers about 100 of the finest looking men we ever saw. Wo unto the enemy that encounters this gallant band of Southern patriots for they will surely 'bite' the dust.

Two months later, Company C, Fifty-fifth Tennessee Infantry Regiment, with Captain John L. McEwen commanding, was organized in Franklin. Rounding out the officer cadre were First Lieutenant John H. Hunter, Second Lieutenant Samuel F. Perkins, and Third Lieutenant James P. Allison. Before the year 1861 was over, a total of nine infantry and two cavalry companies had been raised in Williamson County. All of these companies served with distinction throughout the War and most were not mustered out of Confederate service until after Lee's surrender at Appomattox Courthouse, Virginia, on April 9, 1865.

☆ ☆ ☆

On July 21, 1861, almost within earshot of the nation's capitol, the Union Army, consisting of the largest assemblage of fighting men ever witnessed in North America, encountered an embarrassing defeat at the hands of the Southerners. At a little creek in northern Virginia called Bull Run, during this, the first major conflict of the War, a poorly trained force of thirty-five thousand men and forty-nine guns was decisively humbled by the twenty-two thousand-man, equally ill-trained and equipped Confederate army poised nearby.

Following the disastrous rout, United States officials were desperate for a victory. Bull Run had galvanized politicians and the army high command in Washington as nothing else before had done. Rather than quickly whipping the upstart Rebels and getting on with the nation's business at hand, Yankee army leaders scurried back to the drawing board searching for ways to end the disturbing situation in which they found themselves.

On August 10, 1861, far to the west in Missouri, 5,400 Union soldiers attacked an eleven thousand-man Confederate force. The day again proved disastrous for the Union. Although the losses of 1,317 men for the United States and 1,230 for the Confederates were nearly equal, the victory at Wilson's Creek was decisive for the South. The ensuing Federal retreat left the lower one-third of Missouri in Confederate hands and further damaged the spirits of the

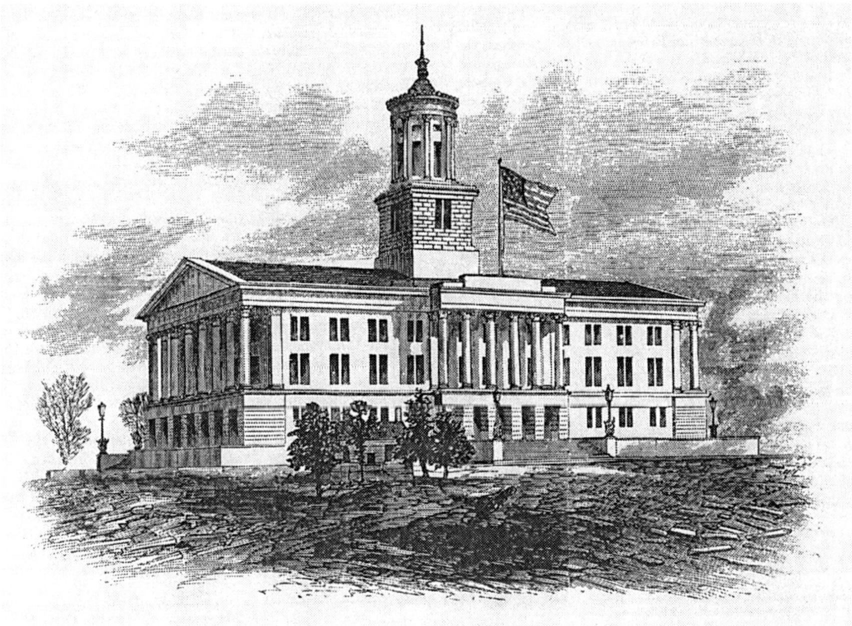

ABOVE
On February 25, 1862, Union troops hoisted the U.S. flag high above the State Capitol in Nashville. From that point until the end of the war, practically all of Middle Tennessee was under Union occupation. (From an old engraving in the collection of James A. Crutchfield)

Union army as the second major conflict of the War ended.

In early 1862, the Federal government, still attempting to make a decisive blow against the Confederacy, made its big play for Tennessee. The strategy was simple. If the Union army occupied Nashville, it would be a logical step to continue heavy troop and supply movement down the long corridor between Nashville and Chattanooga and, then, into the extension of that corridor between Chattanooga and Atlanta. If this plan could be accomplished, the prize city of Atlanta would soon belong to the Union army and the entire Southland would be divided.

On February 25, 1862, Confederate officials at Nashville surrendered the city to the United States Army. Fort Henry, on the Tennessee River guarding the state from the north, had already fallen to Federal troops on February 6, and Fort Donelson, which served an equal function on the Cumberland River, surrendered ten days later. With the capitulation of these two Confederate forts, the state of Tennessee was left totally exposed from the north and became immediate prey for the Union Army.

After the fall of Forts Donelson and Henry and the occupation of Nashville, it grew imperative for the Southern army to take a firm stand in order to halt what promised to be a massive invasion of Middle and West Tennessee. General Albert Sidney Johnston, hoping to do just that, made his way from Nashville to Corinth, Mississippi, and by spring 1862, he had amassed forty-four thousand troops there. Realizing that General Ulysses S. Grant's army, after its victories at the river forts, had followed the Tennessee River to nearby Pittsburg Landing, Johnston was anxious to launch an attack on the forty-thousand-man force before General Don Carlos Buell could reinforce it from Nashville.

Thus, less than two months after Nashville fell to the army of General Buell, the attentions of both the Union and Confederate armies focused on Pittsburg Landing, specifically to the area surrounding a small church called Shiloh. Johnston's Army of Tennessee launched a vicious attack on the morning of April 6, catching all of Grant's command by surprise. Despite early indications that the Confederates would take the day, tables were suddenly turned, General Johnston was killed, Buell arrived from Nashville with fifteen thousand reinforcements, and Johnston's replacement, General P. G. T. Beauregard, ordered a retreat to Corinth. Two months later, Memphis fell, leaving the entire state of Tennessee, except for the eastern part, under Union occupation.

On July 13, 1862, General Nathan Bedford Forrest routed the Union garrison at Murfreesboro and occupied that town. In the meantime, General Braxton Bragg, who had taken command of the Army of Tennessee, attempted to push the Union army out of Tennessee into Kentucky. Failing in his efforts, Bragg fell back to Murfreesboro, where he and his army bivouacked until January 1863 when General William S. Rosecrans and a sizable Union army roared out of Nashville and forced the Confederates to retreat to Chattanooga.

In September 1863, the Army of Tennessee scored one of its most important victories when it defeated General Rosecrans's Union troops at Chickamauga. However, a Confederate failure to follow up on its success allowed Rosecrans to occupy nearby Chattanooga. Later action between the two armies on Missionary Ridge and Lookout Mountain left a defeated Army of Tennessee, now commanded by General Joseph E. Johnston, and large elements of a highly charged Union army under the overall command of General Grant, both drifting slowing southward toward Atlanta.

In March 1864, Grant was promoted to the newly created rank of lieutenant general and placed in charge of all Union armies in all theaters of action. He was replaced in the field by General William Tecumseh Sherman, whose mission now became the occupation of Atlanta. Sherman attacked the city on July 22, thus marking the beginning of a grueling campaign that dragged on until early September, when he telegraphed the War Department in Washington, D.C., that "Atlanta is ours."

The stage was now set for Hood's Tennessee campaign which would hurl his army against a superior Union force at Franklin in late November 1864.

☆ ☆ ☆

From the time of Nashville's occupation in February 1862, until the end of the War, much of the entire Middle Tennessee area, including Franklin and Williamson County, was subject to continuous incursions by Federal troops. Reconnaissance tours, scouting missions, and troop and supply transportation were just a few of the tasks carried out in the region by the men of the United States Army. With Confederate soldiers scattered all over the midstate, it was commonplace for the two foes to meet occasionally.

Skirmishes and other limited actions frequently occurred throughout Williamson County for the duration of the War, culminating, of course, with the Battle of Franklin on November 30, 1864, just weeks after the fall of Atlanta and only five months before the cessation of all hostilities. Although just exactly what constitutes a "military action" is difficult to assess at times, a conservative count indicates that approximately fifty encounters of some magnitude occurred between the combatants within the confines of Williamson County, several of them in the immediate Franklin area. Obviously, in a book this size, all of these actions cannot be documented, but details of some of the more interesting ones are recorded below.

Elements of the Union army first appeared in the area around Franklin during early 1862, concurrent with and following the fall of Forts Donelson and Henry. During mid-March, having secured Nashville, various commands of General Buell's army marched through Franklin on their way to reinforce General Grant at Pittsburg Landing on the Tennessee River. Dr. Samuel Henderson recorded in his diary under the date of March 16, that, "The Federal Army passing through Franklin; ten or twelve thousand passed today." Two days later, Henderson wrote, "Seven or eight thousand passed today."

Only about four hundred Louisiana cavalrymen were on hand to protect the region when Buell approached, and, considering the size of the oncoming army,

ABOVE
During March 1862, thousands of Union soldiers marched through Franklin on their way to reinforce General Ulysses Grant's forces at Pittsburg Landing. (Drawing from Harper's Pictorial History of the Civil War*)*

they quickly disappeared into the surrounding countryside. Mrs. Newton Cannon wrote that:

> . . . it was Sunday morning, and we had gone to Sunday School and had finished with our lessons and were coming out of church when an unusual commotion in the street attracted our attention. On looking down toward the Square, it seemed that the whole heavens had dropped down, so blue were the streets with the blue coated Yankees and it seemed as though the Starry Ground was with them, they were so gay with gold stars and lace. . . . The Southern Army men were in full retreat just ahead of them. On the previous Saturday all day long straggling soldiers were in our dining room refreshing themselves.

Another, unidentified, eyewitness gave the following account of the reactions of Franklin residents to the long lines of Northern soldiers as they marched through the town:

> . . . when the news came that Buell's army would pass through Franklin the next day, everybody was intensely excited and awaited with eagerness its approach, as none had ever seen a live "Yankee" and wondered what they would do when he came.
>
> Bright and early the next morning the cry was heard, "The Yankees have come!" The cavalry had arrived, but found no Confederates lurking behind. Soon after came the infantry, thousands upon thousands, well dressed in new uniforms, bands playing and flags flying—an imposing sight.
>
> While the troops were passing, an officer of pompous mien, with dangling sword and waving plumes, rode up to a group of ladies standing on the steps of the old Dempsey house, at the foot of Main street, and asked one of them, Miss Winnie Nichols, then a blooming lass, but now a dignified matron, "What beautiful stream is that?" referring to Harpeth River. She instantly replied: "That, sir, is second Bull Run, and you are now on your way to second Manassas." At the reply he became furious and livid with rage, but his fellow officers, who heard the repartee and appreciated the wit, exploded with laughter at his discomfiture, and in turn, saluted the young lady, doffing their caps to her.

The next military contingent of any size observed by citizens of Franklin was a Confederate unit, the Eighth Texas Cavalry, sometimes called "Terry's Texas Rangers." Having seen action at Shiloh in April 1862, the regiment, about six hundred strong, passed through the town during the early fall on its way to fight again at Perryville in Kentucky. The Rangers are credited with originating the "Rebel Yell," which would put fear in the hearts of so many Northern soldiers in the years to come. A Union observer once commented that the Rangers were "as quick as lightning," and that "they ride like Arabs, shoot like archers at a mark, and fight like devils." Ironically, the Rangers' dashing commander, Colonel John Austin Wharton, was a native-born Nashvillian, but had been raised and educated in Texas.

At about the same time that Terry's Texas Rangers were frequenting the Franklin area, Union General John M. Palmer—who in later life would become governor of Illinois, United States senator, and unsuccessful presidential candidate against William McKinley in 1896—led his infantry division through the town on his way to Nashville, where he was reassigned to Murfreesboro. When he was on the outskirts of town, Palmer was informed by a Yankee sympathizer that Confederate bushwhackers intended to attack him at Holly Tree Gap, halfway between Franklin and Brentwood. When he arrived in Franklin, Palmer immediately captured several civilians—W. H. Crouch, Ed Sherman, H. P. Fowlkes, Dick Gault, Bob Brown, Mack Craig, Will Ragsdale, Charley Wall, Jim Carr, Dee Crutcher, and brothers T. L. and O. C. Owen—to use as hostages. Marching the outraged men in front of his column, Palmer released them as soon as he and his command were safely through Holly Tree Gap.

In November 1862, after Perryville, General Braxton Bragg began to concentrate his Confederate army around Murfreesboro. In order to provide protection to his front and left flanks, the Fourth Tennessee Cavalry Regiment was assigned outpost duty in Franklin, where it remained until the latter days of the year when it marched to Murfreesboro to take part in the great battle there. According to George B. Guild, the adjutant for the Fourth Tennessee, the men of the regiment, while stationed in Franklin, had "some hot contests with the enemy, killing, wounding, and capturing some, and losing some ourselves." Continuing, Guild wrote that "The enemy made frequent scouts in the neighborhood of Franklin, sometimes resulting in quite a battle." On November 13, the Confederate cavalry destroyed the turnpike bridge over the Harpeth River, thus denying either side its use, including General John M. Schofield's army two years later when it tried to move large numbers of troops rapidly across the river in advance of Hood's army.

On the last day of January 1863, a Union expedition left Murfreesboro under the command of General Jefferson C. Davis (no kin to the Confederacy's president) to reconnoiter a large section of Middle Tennessee. On that day, Davis reported from Eagleville that he would "make Franklin by night to-morrow." The following day, Union General James H. Steedman confirmed that "Colonel Brownlow [J. P.] entered Franklin at 9 o'clock last night, and

ABOVE
Fort Granger was built high atop Figuers' Bluff in order to take command of the surrounding countryside. At its height, the fort garrisoned nearly eight thousand Union infantry and cavalry troops. (Drawing from The Confederate Soldier in the Civil War*)*

learned that the enemy had gone in the direction of Harpeth Shoals." Steedman reported that only one man was lost in the occupation.

On February 3, Confederate General Gideon Pillow, a former law partner of James K. Polk and a decorated Mexican War veteran, notified General Joseph Wheeler from Columbia of the latest action in the area. He advised Wheeler that "The enemy now occupy Franklin," adding that "It is said to be Jefferson C. Davis, about 8,000 or 9,000 strong, and one regiment of cavalry, about 400 strong." Continuing, Pillow reported that the Franklin bridge over the Harpeth River was in the process of being rebuilt by the Union infantry, which was "on the north side of the river." Davis returned to Murfreesboro on February 13.

During the late winter of 1863, the Union high command in Nashville dispatched General Gordon Granger to Franklin to occupy the town and to build a strong fortification that would house and protect the sizable garrison that was to be placed there. Granger's chief of engineers, Captain W. E. Merrill, selected Figuers' Bluff, a limestone outcropping that rose some sixty feet above the Harpeth River and the surrounding flood plain, for the fort's site. Merrill's men built a three-sided earthen structure, with one side poised on the precipice that dropped off to the river below. The remaining two sides consisted of ten-feet-deep, sixteen-feet-wide trenches that ran alongside the walls that were made from the dirt excavated from the ditches. The walls themselves averaged about six to eight feet in height and ran for some nine hundred feet around the fort's interior grounds.

ROPER'S KNOB

When the Union Army fortified Figuers' Bluff in early 1863, engineers also placed a signal station atop nearby Roper's Knob, located just off today's Franklin Pike and Mark Hatcher Parkway. Roper's was only one of six smaller redoubts placed atop high hills or on otherwise prominent elevations to the north and east of Franklin. Park Marshall, one-time mayor of Franklin, as well as of Nashville, was a lad of seven or eight years old when the forts were built, and in his history of Franklin, written in 1917, he describes Roper's Knob.

A man named Roper lived a great many years on Roper's Knob, but he does not seem to have owned the land. His house was jam-up against the top knob but on the flat space next to the knob or upper part. Some of its foundation and chimney stones are still there.

Somewhere not far away the Long Hunter and pioneer, Thomas Sharpe Spencer (Big Foot Spencer) owned a tract of 320 acres. . . . I think that land must have been a mile or two above Roper's Knob on the creek which took its name from the Spencers.

Among surprising things that were said in the early days of the Civil War was one by an old lady neighbor of ours. She came to see our family to tell us that the Yankees were going to put a gunboat on the top of Roper's Knob. The Yankees indeed were busy out there. They cut down all the trees but left a pear tree about half way up the upper knob. They built a large fort covering the whole top of the knob and a strong line of rock and earth works all the way around, and half-way up the upper knob, the remains of both of which are still there. The pear tree stands till today in this line of works, old as it is. They constructed a tramway from the nearly level space, or "bench," to the fort at the top of the Knob. It had heavy crossties and heavy square wooden beams for the rails. An engine and derrick were installed with ropes and drum to draw up heavy artillery with which the fort was supplied. A large horizontal limb from the pear tree extended over this tramway; the scar where this limb rotted off is still there. After a time the Yankees covered the entire fort with a roof. Right at the foot of the upper Knob and on its N. W. side are several large stones that look like the upper work of a cistern there to which water from the roof was carried.

Roper's Knob, as also was Fort Granger, was a signal station—signaling by wig-way by day, and by colored fire balls by night, to Nashville, and to a line of stations to Murfreesboro. The fort was not garrisoned at the time the battle [of Franklin in November 1864] was fought.

Several prominent features dominated the inside of the fort. A long "blast" wall—constructed of brick taken from the nearby Harpeth Male Academy and designed to trap incoming artillery shells, along with a powder magazine built on the top of the basement of a long-ago deserted house—occupied the center of the compound. A cistern trapped and held nine thousand gallons of water. Thirty-five cannon emplacements encircled the top of the walls, and rifle pits that provided a place from which infantrymen could fire at an advancing enemy were dug just outside the fort on the approach that faced the Harpeth River. The length of the fort was crowned by sharpened pickets which deterred would-be attackers from scaling the fort's sloping walls.

☆ ☆ ☆

On April 10, 1863, in far-off Richmond, Virginia, Confederate President Jefferson Davis issued the following proclamation which gave his support to the congressional ban on growing cotton and tobacco on Southern farms in favor of food crops that would support the army.

> Let fields be devoted exclusively to the production of corn, oats, beans, peas, potatoes, and other food for man and beast; let corn be sown broadcast for fodder . . . and let all your efforts be directed to the prompt supply of these articles in the districts where our armies are operating. . . . Alone, unaided, we have met and overthrown the most formidable combination of naval and military armaments that the lust of conquest ever gathered together for the subjugation of a free people. . . . We must not forget, however, that the war is not yet ended, and that we are still confronted by powerful armies and threatened by numerous fleets; and that the Government which controls these fleets and armies is driven to the most desperate efforts to effect the unholy purposes in which it has thus far been defeated.

On the same day that President Davis was outlawing nonfood agricultural production throughout the Confederacy, local residents, as well as General Gordon Granger and the Union troops inside Fort Granger, were bracing themselves for a rumored attack on Franklin. Around noon, Confederate General Earl Van Dorn, who had been reconnoitering the region for some time, swarmed up from the south and east with nine thousand cavalrymen and mounted infantrymen, supplemented by two regiments of infantry. Fort Granger was still incomplete at the time, and the total Union strength in Franklin consisted only of "5,194 infantry, 2,728 cavalry, eighteen pieces of artillery, and two siege guns. . . ." The siege guns, both twenty-four pounders, were located inside the fort and were mounted on swivels so that their crew could direct fire in any direction.

General Granger recorded in his official report, written from Franklin on April 15, that:

> Friday, the 10th instant, was a dark, smoky, and windy day. The dust was blown from Franklin and from the dry roads directly into our faces, which, together with the condition of the atmosphere, so obstructed our vision that we could scarcely distinguish a fence from a line of horsemen, even with our field glasses, at the distance of over 1 mile. For the enemy it was a most propitious day for an attack.

Van Dorn's army moved up the Columbia Pike from Spring Hill. When the column passed through the gap between Winstead and Breezy Hills, they divided, with half cutting cross-country to the Lewisburg Pike and the remainder following the Columbia Pike. As the Columbia Pike contingent of Van Dorn's troops neared the Carter family cotton gin, Granger ordered the big siege guns in the fort to fire upon them. The Confederates returned the fire with their own rifled cannon with little effect. In the meantime, Granger misread Van Dorn's movements, and, thinking that his real objective was the small Union garrison at Brentwood, sent all of his cavalry off in that direction. Learning too late that Van Dorn's goal really was the occupation of Franklin, Granger regrouped his remaining troops and attempted to hold off the Confederates, who attacked in force. As darkness rapidly approached, Van Dorn pushed the Union soldiers back, but then withdrew and retreated toward Spring Hill.

On June 4, 1863, cavalrymen under the command of General Nathan Bedford Forrest unsuccessfully attempted to make amends for Van Dorn's earlier failure to take Franklin from Union hands. At 3:00 P.M., several thousand Confederates rode into town amidst heavy artillery fire from Fort Granger. As Captain

ABOVE
This contemporary artist's rendition of the hanging of the two Confederate spies at Franklin in June 1863 made the front page of Harper's Weekly.

Henry Smith and several other Southern officers discussed the situation on Main Street, they were bombarded by artillery fire. Smith later wrote that the ". . . shelling was terrific from Figuers's Hill where the great federal forts were erected and in crossing the Public Square a twenty-pound shell exploded killing and wounding several horses and a few men." Two days after the initial Confederate attempt to occupy Franklin, the fort's commander, Colonel John P. Baird of the Eighty-fifth Indiana Infantry—General Granger in the meantime having been transferred to Triune—reported that "I am satisfied they will attack within twenty-four hours, as they are hovering about." Baird's fears were unfounded, however, and the Confederates' second try at occupying Franklin in as many months ended in failure.

☆ ☆ ☆

Four days after General Forrest's aborted attempt to reclaim Franklin for the Confederacy, two men rode into Fort Granger and identified themselves to Colonel Baird as Colonel Austin and Major Dunlap of the United States inspector general's staff. The two men told Baird that their mission was the inspection of the many far-flung Union forts and outposts in the area. When Baird asked to see the pair's official orders, they quickly produced papers that appeared to bear a genuine signature of General William Rosecrans, the Union commander at Murfreesboro, as well as documents from the War Department in Washington that explained their assignment in the region.

An unnamed surgeon of the Eighty-fifth Indiana Infantry Regiment wrote an article about the two men for *Harper's Magazine,* which appeared one month after the affair. In the piece, the physician described the two strangers as wearing:

> . . . citizens' overcoats, Federal regulation pants and caps. The caps were covered with white flannel havelocks. They wore side arms, and showed high intelligence. . . . They asked the Colonel to loan them $50, as they had no coats and no money to buy them. Colonel Baird loaned them the money, and took Colonel Austin's note for it.

As the sun was going down, the two officers announced that they must be on their way to Nashville. No sooner had they left Fort Granger than Colonel Baird, having second thoughts about their legitimacy, dispatched two men to chase them down and return them to Franklin. The two had not gone far before they were

KEEPING ORDER IN FRANKLIN

During the months that the Union Army actively occupied Franklin, Yankee authorities in the town were constantly releasing orders to their men, admonishing them to respect private rights, give receipts for commandeered property, and to refrain from drinking and gambling. Below is a sampling of general orders issued by the commandant at Fort Granger during the months of July and August 1863.

HEAD QUARTERS U.S. FORCES
FRANKLIN, TENN, JULY 4TH 1863
General Orders, No.3.

No officers or enlisted man will be permitted to leave his camp, without a pass from his commanding officer.

No person will be allowed to cross the Grand Guard line or river without a pass from Major Generals Rosecrans or Granger; Brigade Generals Morgan or Granger; and the Provost Marshal.

Any officer or enlisted man found drunk, trespassing upon private premises, using insulting language to any citizen or out of camp without a proper pass, will be arrested instantly by the Patrol Guard.

No person will be admitted inside the works of Fort Granger or "Roper Knob," except the officers and men assigned to duty at the respective points.

All pieces will be discharged daily between the hours of 12 P.M. and 1 PM. Any person discharging arms at any other hour will be promptly arrested.

No negroes [sic] will be allowed within the camp lines except those actually employed.

HEAD QUARTERS, U.S. FORCES
FRANKLIN, TENN., JULY 19, '63
General Orders, No.7.

It having come to the knowledge of the Colonel commanding, that gambling is practiced to a greater or less extent at this post. It is hereby ordered that all games for money or its equivalent, is strictly prohibited. Rigorous measures will be taken to prevent it. Any one belonging in this command found indulging in this vice will be arrested and severely punished.

This order will forthwith be published to every company and detachment of this command.

HEAD QUARTERS U.S. FORCES
FRANKLIN, TENN. AUG. 6TH 1863
General Orders, NO. 9.

The Colonel Commanding has learned with regret that men of his Command have in several instances visited private residence without invitation asking music from the inmates. This practice must cease.

The Provost Guard will freely patrol the streets, arresting any soldier without a proper pass, in a private residence without invitation with or without a pass, or conducting themselves in an improper manner, and place them in the jail for punishment.

HEAD QUARTERS U.S. FORCES
FRANKLIN, TENN, AUG. 6TH, 1863
General Orders, No. 10.

The Colonel Commanding has learned that horses and mules have been seized and no receipts given therefore. The Government of the United States will not tolerate such conduct but will severely punish the offenders.

The people of that portion of Tennessee within my jurisdiction must rest assured that complete vouchers will be given for any horse or mule and all forage seized for the use of this command. All persons who have received vouchers for property will immediately report the fact to these Head Quarters.

overtaken by their pursuers. Riding back to the fort, no mention was made of an arrest, the premise for their return being that Baird wanted to question them further.

After a few minutes of conversation with the men, Baird convinced himself that Austin and Dunlap were not Union inspectors. He telegraphed General Rosecrans in Murfreesboro, asking him if he had authorized any such mission. When Rosecrans's reply came back negative, Baird arrested the pair and charged them with being Confederate spies. Searching them, Baird discovered that Dunlap carried a Confederate sword. Their cover now blown, Austin and Dunlap confessed to being Confederates whose real names were Colonel Lawrence Williams, who sometimes went by the last name of Orton, and Lieutenant W. G. Peter.

When Baird telegraphed Rosecrans again for guidance on how to handle the situation, he was told "to try them by a drum-head court-martial, and if found guilty hang them immediately." The trial was held during the early morning hours of June 9. Not surprisingly, Williams and Peter were found guilty and sentenced to hang. The prisoners received last rites by a chaplain of the Seventy-eighth Illinois Volunteers and were given a few minutes to write letters to relatives and friends and to dispose of their personal belongings.

"The gallows was constructed by a wild cherry-tree not far from the depot, and in a very public place," wrote the Indiana surgeon in his article for *Harper's*. Continuing, he revealed that "A little after nine o'clock A.M. the whole garrison was marshaled around the place of execution in solemn sadness." Two coffins made from local poplar wood were laid out on the ground, and at 9:20, "the guards conducted the prisoners to the scaffold. . . ."

After being blindfolded, the two spies were placed on a cart, which promptly at 9:30 was driven away leaving the men dangling by their necks. "What a fearful penalty!" lamented the physician. Thirty minutes later, the bodies were cut down and examined, and the men were pronounced dead.

> The Colonel was buried with a gold locket and chain on his neck. The locket contained the portrait and a braid of hair of his intended wife—her portrait was also in his vest pocket—these were buried with him. Both men were buried in the same grave—companions in life, misfortune, and crime, companions in infamy, and now companions in the grave.

☆ ☆ ☆

Franklin and Fort Granger remained relatively peaceful for the remainder of 1863 and most of 1864. An inspection report written in December 1863 revealed that:

> Fort [Granger] is in very good condition. The magazine is large and leaks badly, but a shed was being built over it to try to keep it dry. The ammunition did not seem to be damaged from dampness, it being frequently taken out and aired. The magazine is used as a commissary storehouse as well as to keep ammunition.
>
> The fort is armed with one thirty-pounder Parrott, two rifled twenty-four pounders and three howitzers; another eight inch howitzer is in a small work a few hundred yards inside the fort; they drill well. Military appearance, care of guns and implements and police very good. The garrison, consisting of two companies of the 14th Michigan Infantry, are also quartered inside the fort.

Little by little, both the garrison and the big guns at Fort Granger were evacuated, and by November 30, 1864, when Generals John Bell Hood and John M. Schofield fought it out at Franklin, the fortification had fallen into decay and served no purpose other than that selected by Schofield for his own command's use.

The Battle of Franklin 1864

GENERAL JOSEPH JOHNSTON'S failure to contain the aggressive General William Tecumseh Sherman at Atlanta during the fall of 1864 resulted in his replacement as commander of the Army of Tennessee by General John Bell Hood. Following the expulsion of the Confederates and the occupation of the city by Sherman, Hood devised the idea that he would swing back north, through Alabama and into Tennessee, and attempt to recapture Nashville. Along the way, he would destroy the Nashville and Chattanooga Railroad, which was indispensable for Sherman's success in the Deep South. Hood contemplated that if this strategy was successful, it would be just a matter of time before his army marched to and crossed the Ohio River and raised havoc with the Yankees in their own territory.

Hood discussed the idea with his superior, General P. G. T. Beauregard, at Gadsden, Alabama, in October. Obtaining approval for the plan, he led his large army, numbering between thirty and forty thousand men, into Tennessee. In the meantime, Sherman had dispatched General George Thomas from Atlanta with orders to take over the Union command at Nashville. He also transferred Generals John M. Schofield and David S. Stanley back north to reinforce Thomas. By the middle of November, during unseasonably cold and icy weather, Schofield and his Twenty-third Corps, along with Stanley's Fourth Corps, had been moved to Pulaski. By November 24, in advance of Hood's northward movement, they had fallen back toward Columbia. There, the two corps, totaling nearly twenty-one thousand men, were bivouacked when Hood and the Army of Tennessee approached the area from Alabama.

At around noon on November 29, elements of both armies met at Spring Hill, located fifteen miles south of Franklin. A spirited engagement followed, resulting in nearly one thousand casualties, both Union and Confederate. Then, during the late evening of the twenty-ninth, an incident that has been described by historians as "one of the most controversial non-fighting events of the entire war," occurred on the outskirts of the same little village. Earlier in the day, Schofield, in overall command of the combined Union army, had received a dispatch from General Thomas at Nashville ordering him to maintain his position along the Duck River for as long as possible. However, if he was forced to fall back, then he was to march to Franklin and hold his line at the Harpeth River. The delaying action on Schofield's part would give Thomas ample time to strengthen his forces at Nashville and to align them for Hood's upcoming assault.

The "affair" at Spring Hill occurred when Schofield's army finally did undertake the march toward Nashville during the evening of November 29. According to Hood's later memoirs, he, Hood, arrived in the Spring Hill area about 3:00 P.M., and "sitting upon my horse, I had in sight the enemy's wagons and men passing at double-quick along the Franklin pike." Hood wrote that he ordered General Benjamin Franklin Cheatham to "Go with your Corps, take possession of and hold that pike at or near Spring Hill." Hood also admonished General Patrick Cleburne to "Go with General Cheatham, assist him in every way you can, and do as he directs." Cheatham later denied that any troop movement occurred in the region at 3:00 P.M. and alleged that "General Hood's memory proved treacherous."

Historians have never fully decided what really happened at Spring Hill on the evening of November 29, and this book is not the place to delve into the incident in detail. Regardless of the circumstances, however, the foremost fact is that a huge tactical error was committed by Hood when he allowed Schofield to move around his own command and to place itself between him and Franklin. When Hood awoke on the morning of the thirtieth to find that the enemy had completely bypassed his army, he was furious, and in the words of one of his lieutenants, as "wrathy as a rattlesnake." In his memoirs, Hood freely blamed others of his staff for the debacle, but Schofield wrote of the event that:

> He [Hood] thought he was going to 'catch me napping,' after the tactics of Stonewall Jackson, while in fact I was watching him all day. Besides, Hood went to bed that night, while I was in the saddle all night, directing

ABOVE
This is the scene that General Schofield's army saw on the morning of November 30, 1864, when it hurried toward Franklin after thwarting Hood's army at Spring Hill the night before. (Drawing from Battles and Leaders of the Civil War*)*

> in person all the important movements of my troops. Perhaps that is enough to account for the difference between success and failure, without censuring subordinate commanders.

☆ ☆ ☆

General Schofield and his staff arrived in Franklin at 3:00 A.M. on November 30. They found the town to consist of between fifteen hundred and two thousand residents, most of them living or operating businesses in the sixteen square block area that made up the original town or in the "subdivisions" of Hincheyville and Bell Town.

General Jacob Cox commandeered the home of Fountain B. Carter, "the last house in the suburbs of the town, on the Columbia pike," to serve as temporary headquarters for the combined Fourth and Twenty-third Corps.

ABOVE
Major General John M. Schofield, the Union commander at the Battle of Franklin. (Photo from Miller's Photographic History of the Civil War*)*

Upon reconnoitering the area, Schofield was disappointed to discover that the turnpike bridge over the Harpeth River on the Nashville Pike had been destroyed and that the railroad bridge over the same stream had been severely damaged by fire. Although he had never seriously contemplated a fight at Franklin, it quickly became apparent to him that it would be impossible to get his thousands of troops across the Harpeth and on their way to Nashville before Hood's rapidly advancing army caught up with him from behind. It was then that he realized that he must dig in, fortify his southern approaches as well as possible, make haste in repairing the bridges, and prepare for a spirited encounter with Hood.

As soon as the Union engineers arrived, Schofield set them to work on extending and improving the several hundred yards of earthworks located in the southern part of town that were left in the neighborhood from previous campaigns. "The Federal soldiers were at once put to work constructing fortifications entirely around the south margin of the town," wrote an excited fifteen-year-old Franklin boy, Hardin Figuers. Continuing, the lad exclaimed, "They worked like beavers, using houses, fences, timber and dirt." When the defensive works were completed later in the day, they extended from the Harpeth River near the Lewisburg Pike all the way around the southern and western approaches to Franklin and to the river again on the northern edge of town.

In the meantime, Schofield personally supervised his army's preparations for the attack that he knew the enraged Hood would soon make. Captain Levi T. Scofield, an engineer on Schofield's staff, later wrote that:

> It was deemed expedient by General Schofield to make our stand on the south side of the town and river, so that the trains could mass in the streets and open spaces in the village, while a wagon-road bridge was being built and planks laid on the sleepers of the railroad bridge for their transfer across. . . . There was nothing to do but construct the bridges with the meager facilities at hand; so, with his Engineer Battalion and details of troops, the work was performed,

> requiring the General's constant personal attention. He remained in this position up to the time of the engagement, so as to better superintend the crossing, and at the same time be near the railroad and telegraph station; while from Fort Granger, on the bluff east of the railroad and near the river, he had perfect command during the battle of the entire field, and to direct the fire of the artillery stationed there with him.

As the morning grew longer, on and on came the Union troops. Forward progress had slowed since the march had begun at Spring Hill the night before, because now, General Nathan Bedford Forrest's cavalrymen continually pestered Schofield's men whenever they found a straggling unit or a gap in the column. When the advance guard of the Fourth and Twenty-third Corps approached town, Schofield sent one division of infantry marching straight through Franklin and across the still bridgeless Harpeth River and ordered its commander to prepare to defend the northern side of the stream. Several pieces of artillery were installed and manned in the otherwise deserted Fort Granger.

The men of the infantry regiments spread out behind the earthworks all the way from Lewisburg Pike, through the Carter family property, across Main and Fair Streets, and back to the Harpeth River near the present-day Farmers' Market. When other units of the Union Army rode into Franklin later in the morning and early afternoon, they found, in the words of a member of the Sixty-fourth Ohio Infantry Regiment, "a strong line of works . . . not only strongly built, but . . . well manned. . . ."

At a little before 3:00 P.M., Schofield received a message from General Thomas at Nashville asking him if he could "hold Hood at Franklin for three days longer. . . ." Schofield dispatched a reply stating, "I do not believe I can." By then, Hood's army had already pulled up to the southern part of town, and Schofield, fearing the worst, had prepared his two corps for an extended attack. "He [Hood] now has a large force . . . in my front. . . . A worst position than this for an inferior force could hardly be found," he ruefully added.

☆ ☆ ☆

Most of the elements of Hood's Army of Tennessee left Spring Hill at dawn on November 30, hard on the heels of Schofield's troops. By now, the weather had turned warm again, and the day was summerlike and balmy.

Travel was relatively easy for man, beast, and wagon. But easy travel did not detract from the unhappiness of the men and officers of Hood's command. The eminent historian of the War Between the States, Stanley F. Horn, paints a vivid word picture of what the movement must have been like in his book, *Tennessee's War*:

> Probably no army ever marched to battle in such a temper as pervaded the Army of Tennessee that morning, plodding along the dusty road from Spring Hill to Franklin, fifteen miles away. The army's commander was disappointed and angry; his subordinates were in equally bad humor; and the feeling of frustration had permeated the ranks and engendered in the men as well as the officers a resolution to overtake and whip the enemy who had slipped through their fingers the preceding night.

At noon, General Hood and advance elements of his army arrived at the Harrison House, located on the south side of Winstead Hill about two miles from Franklin. There, he found elements of Union General George D. Wagner's Second Infantry Division occupying the highlands between the Harrison House and Franklin. Dispatching part of General A. P. Stewart's Infantry Corps to dislodge Wagner, Hood settled down with his staff in the commandeered Harrison House and began to lay plans for the next step in his offensive campaign.

At around 1:00 P.M., Hood and several staff officers rode to the top of the 840-feet-high Winstead Hill, located west of the Columbia Pike, to personally view Schofield's strategic endeavors. What they saw was mind-boggling. Stretched before them for as far as they could see were the complex lines of defensive earthworks that encircled Franklin from riverbank to riverbank. Through their field glasses they could see the artillery emplacements inside Fort Granger, perched atop Figuers' Bluff on the far side of the Harpeth River.

General Cheatham exclaimed that he did not "like the looks of the fight," and General Forrest literally begged Hood to withhold a frontal attack until his own cavalrymen had a chance to cross the Harpeth north of town and attack Schofield from the rear. Others of Hood's staff reminded the general that one complete corps and all of the artillery were still moving up the road from Spring Hill and that they would not arrive for hours. In the meantime, General Pat Cleburne, observing the Union works from his vantage point atop Merrill's Hill, gasped, "They have three lines of works, and they are all completed!"

All of Hood's staff officers' lamentations fell on deaf ears. Sergeant Major S. A. Cunningham, who after the War became the moving spirit behind, and the editor of, the widely respected *Confederate Veteran Magazine,* was within earshot

ABOVE
Major General Benjamin Franklin Cheatham was the highest ranking native Nashvillian to serve in the Confederate Army. Just prior to the Battle of Franklin, he told General Hood that he did not like the looks of the fight, a remark that went unheeded by Hood. After the War, Hood blamed Cheatham for the debacle at Spring Hill, a charge that was totally unfounded. (Drawing from McGee's History of Tennessee)

of the generals during their arguments over whether to attack Schofield or not. He later wrote that:

> I watched him [Hood] closely, meditating upon his responsibility. When he returned to the top of the hill and near where I happened to be standing, a general officer . . . met him and Hood said, "General, we will make the fight," and the two clasped hands. Orders were speedily dispatched to various commanders.

ABOVE
Major General Nathan Bedford Forrest pleaded with General Hood to delay his attack on Schofield until his cavalry units could cross the Harpeth River and strike the Union army from behind. Like Cheatham's entreaties, Forrest's were ignored as well. (Drawing from McGee's History of Tennessee*)*

Less than two hours after Hood made his monumental decision to frontally assault Schofield's well-laid defenses, most of General Cheatham's corps had arrived from Spring Hill and were marching along the Columbia Pike through the gap that separated Winstead and Breezy Hills. Cheatham, himself a native Nashvillian and the great-grandson of the city's founder, James Robertson, commanded thirty regiments of Tennesseans, as well as those of other Southern states, in his corps. When the long columns of Tennessee infantry cleared the gap and saw Franklin in front of them, they must have temporarily forgotten that two corps of the Union's finest fighting men still separated them from their loved ones.

☆ ☆ ☆

No two men could have been more different in their physical appearance, their philosophies, and their attitudes toward life and warfare than John Bell Hood and John McAllister Schofield, the two adversaries on the field of battle at Franklin. Although they both graduated from West Point Academy in the same year, 1853, Schofield finished seventh and Hood finished forty fourth out of a class of fifty-four graduates. During his senior year at West Point, Hood came very near to being expelled due to the number of demerits, 196, that he had received during his four years there.

Both men were born in 1831, Hood four months the senior. Hood was a Kentuckian, the epitome of the agrarian-influenced "southern gentleman," while Schofield hailed from New York, was raised in Illinois, and reflected his middle-class upbringing as the son of a Baptist preacher. Hood stood six feet, two inches tall, all packed in a lean, muscular frame, while Schofield was considerably shorter and more heavyset. Hood liked to gamble, drink, and take chances, while Schofield was more reserved, was the typical "hard worker," and refrained from vices. In their book, *Five Tragic Hours,* a volume that remains the best generalized work on the Battle of Franklin, authors James Lee McDonough and the late Thomas L. Connelly succinctly explained the differences between Hood and Schofield when they wrote, "If Hood was aggressive, emotional, romantic, and a dreamer, Schofield was articulate, calm, reflective, and dispassionate, his subtle sense of humor virtually hidden from all except those few who knew him intimately."

Despite the differences, the two men had a high regard for each other while students at West Point, and afterwards. Reminiscing on his military academy days, Schofield once recalled that Hood was

> a jolly good fellow, a little discouraged at first by unexpected hard work; but he fought his way manfully to the end. He was not quite so talented as some of his great associates in the Confederate army, but he was a tremendous fighter when occasion offered. Hood was not well up in mathematics. The first part of the course he found very hard—so much so that he became discouraged and seemed much depressed. He asked me which I would prefer to be, "an officer of the army or a farmer in Kentucky?" I replied in

> a way which aroused his ambition to accomplish what he had set out to do in coming to West Point, without regard to preference between farming and soldiering. He went to work in good earnest, and passed the January examination, though by a very narrow margin. From that time on he did not seem to have so much difficulty. When we were fighting each other so desperately, fifteen years later, I wondered whether Hood remembered the encouragement I had given him to become a soldier, and came very near thinking once or twice that perhaps I had made a mistake. But I do not believe that public enmity ever diminished my personal regard for my old friend and classmate.

After leaving West Point, Hood accepted his commission with the infantry and was sent to California. Fifteen months later, he transferred to the cavalry and to Texas to help protect the frontier from marauding Comanches. It was in Texas that he first became friends with several future Confederate leaders with whom he would later have strong ties, including Robert E. Lee and Albert Sidney Johnston. When most of the Southern states seceded from the Union, Hood resigned his commission in the United States Army and accepted one in the Confederate forces, rising all the way to lieutenant general by 1864. Along the way though, he had lost the use of one arm at Gettysburg and a leg to amputation at Chickamauga. By the time he arrived at Franklin, he was only the shadow of the warrior he had once been.

When Schofield graduated from the U.S. Military Academy, he received a second lieutenant's commission with an artillery regiment, served in Florida for a while, then taught at his alma mater, West Point. He later became a civilian instructor at Washington University in St. Louis, where he resided when the War Between the States broke out. In August 1861, at Wilson's Creek, as a major with the First Missouri Infantry Regiment, Schofield displayed exemplary courage, for which he was later awarded a Medal of Honor. Promotions to brigadier general, then major general of U.S. Volunteers soon followed. Ironically, Schofield was promoted to brigadier general in the regular U.S. Army on November 30, 1864, the same day he and Hood exchanged blows at Franklin.

The later careers of Hood and Schofield were just as opposite each other as their earlier ones had been. After the War, Hood, a physical wreck, retired to New Orleans where he eventually entered business enjoying nominal success as a merchant and as the president of the Louisiana branch of the Life Association of America. He, along with his wife and oldest child, died during the great yellow fever epidemic of 1879. Schofield went on to succeed Edwin Stanton as U.S. secretary of war in President Andrew Johnson's administration, and afterwards served as commander of various army districts throughout the country. From 1876 to 1880, he saw service as superintendent of the U.S. Military Academy, and from 1888 to 1895 as commander-in-chief of the U.S. Army. Schofield died in 1906, having been promoted to lieutenant general before his retirement eleven years earlier.

☆ ☆ ☆

At a few minutes past 3:00 P.M. on November 30, 1864, the Kentucky, Indiana, Ohio, and Illinois farm boys who made up the majority of General Schofield's Union army at Franklin, peered southward over the miles of breastworks and beheld a sight that most of them had never witnessed before. Streaming along the Columbia Pike through the gap between Winstead and Breezy Hills, more than 100 regiments of Confederate infantry troops, augmented by artillery and cavalry units, burst forth upon the lowlands leading toward Franklin. Regimental bands alternated playing "Dixie," "The Girl I Left Behind," and "Bonnie Blue Flag," and divisional banners and guidons waved in the wind.

General Jacob Cox, the commander of the Third Division of the Twenty-third Corps and Schofield's second-in-command, was surveying troops in a trench near the Carter House when he looked to the south and saw "the enemy . . . as a dark line coming diagonally down Winstead Hill, blotting out the white streak of the turnpike. . . ." Cox correctly predicted that "Hood must attack soon or not at all."

Most of the enlisted men and many of the officers on both sides had difficulty believing that a Confederate attack had been ordered upon the well-entrenched Union Army at all, much less one that would begin at such a late hour in the day. Schofield himself, apparently not too worried that Hood would strike, had already moved his headquarters from the Carter House to the Alpheus Truett place, north of the Harpeth River, in anticipation of moving his troops toward Nashville during the night. By now, the sun was rapidly setting behind the hills west of Franklin, and it would be only another hour or so before darkness would envelope the countryside. But, two miles south of town, among Hood's corps commanders, orders to prepare for an immediate charge were circulating from regiment to regiment.

The majority of Hood's army were seasoned veterans. Many had fought at Shiloh, Murfreesboro, Chickamauga, Chattanooga, and Atlanta. The

EYEWITNESS TO THE BATTLE OF FRANKLIN: A SOLDIER'S VIEW

Private Sam Watkins of Columbia, Tennessee, served in Company H, 1st Tennessee Regiment (the Maury Grays) of the Army of Tennessee for the entire duration of the War between the States and saw action in every major battle in which the army participated. Of the 120 men who originally joined the Maury Grays at Columbia in 1861, only Sam and six other individuals were left at the War's end in 1865.

In 1881–1882, Watkins recalled his harrowing War experiences in a series of newspaper articles for the Columbia *Herald.* A short time afterwards, he published the pieces in book form under the title, *Co. "Aytch," A Side Show of the Big Show.* Watkins's recollections are a gold mine of information about the Army of Tennessee, its dedicated soldiers and leaders, and the battles in which they fought.

As the war was winding down in Tennessee, Sam's unit was poised at Franklin on the last day of November 1864, just in time for the big battle. This son of Tennessee told in his own eloquent words his impressions of that dismal and never-to-be forgotten day.

> *Kind reader, right here my pen, and courage, and ability fail me. I shrink from butchery. Would to God I could tear the page from these memoirs and from my own memory. It is the blackest page in the history of the war of the Lost Cause. It was the bloodiest battle of modern times in any war. It was the finishing stroke to the independence of the Southern Confederacy. I was there. I saw it. My flesh trembles, and creeps, and crawls when I think of it today. My heart almost ceases to beat at the horrid recollection. Would to God that I had never witnessed such a scene!*
>
> *I cannot describe it. It beggars description. I will not attempt to describe it. I could not. The death-angel was there to gather its last harvest. It was the grand coronation of death. Would that I could turn the page. But I feel, though I did so, that page would still be there, teeming with its scenes of horror and blood. I can only tell of what I saw.*
>
> *Our regiment was resting in the gap of a range of hills in plain view of the city of Franklin. We could see the battleflags of the enemy waving in the breeze. Our army had been depleted of its strength by a forced march from Spring Hill, and stragglers lined the road. Our artillery had not yet come up, and could not be brought into action. Our cavalry was across Harpeth river, and our army was but in poor condition to make an assault. While resting on this hill-side, I saw a courier dash up to our commanding general, B. F. Cheatham, and the word, "Attention!" was given. I knew then that we would soon be in action. Forward, march. We passed over the hill and through a little skirt of woods.*

The enemy were fortified right across the Franklin pike, in the suburbs of the town. Right here in these woods a detail of skirmishers was called for. Our regiment was detailed. We deployed as skirmishers, firing as we advanced on the left of the turnpike road. If I had not been a skirmisher on that day, I would not have been writing this today, in the year of our Lord 1882.

It was four o'clock on that dark and dismal . . . day when the line of battle was formed, and those devoted heroes were ordered forward. . . .

As they marched on down through an open field toward the rampart of blood and death, the Federal batteries began to open and mow down and gather into the garner of death, as brave, and good, and pure spirits as the world ever saw. The twilight of evening had begun to gather as a precursor of the coming blackness of midnight darkness that was to envelop a scene so sickening and horrible that it is impossible for me to describe it. "Forward, men," is repeated all along the line. A sheet of fire was poured into our very faces, and for a moment we halted as if in despair, as the terrible avalanche of shot and shell laid low those brave and gallant heroes, whose bleeding wounds attested that the struggle would be desperate. Forward, men! The air loaded with death-dealing missiles. Never on this earth did men fight against such terrible odds. It seemed that the very elements of heaven and earth were in one mighty uproar. Forward, men! And the blood spurts in a perfect jet from the dead and wounded. The earth is red with blood. It runs in streams, making little rivulets as it flows. Occasionally there was a little lull in the storm of battle, as the men were loading their guns, and for a few moments it seemed as if night tried to cover the scene with her mantle. The death-angel shrieks and laughs and old Father Time is busy with his sickle, as he gathers in the last harvest of death, crying, More, more, more! while his rapacious maw is glutted with the slain.

But the skirmish line being deployed out, extending a little wider than the battle did—passing through a thicket of small locusts, where Brown, orderly sergeant of Company B, was killed—we advanced on toward the breastworks, on and on. I had made up my mind to die—felt glorious. We pressed forward until I heard the terrific roar of battle open on our right. Cleburne's division was charging their works. I passed on until I got to their works, and got over on their (the Yankees') side. But in fifty yards of where I was the scene was lit up by fires that seemed like hell itself. It appeared to be but one line of streaming fire. Our troops were upon one side of the breastworks, and the Federals on the other. I ran up on the line of works, where our men were engaged. Dead soldiers filled the entrenchments. The firing was kept up until after midnight, and gradually died out. We passed the night where we were. But when the morrow's sun began to light up the eastern sky with its rosy hues, and we looked over the battlefield, O, my God!

what did we see! It was a grand holocaust of death. Death had held high carnival there that night. The dead were piled the one on the other all over the ground. I never was so horrified and appalled in my life. Horses, like men, had died game on the gory breastworks. General Adams' horse had his fore feet on one side of the works and his hind feet on the other, dead. The general seems to have been caught so that he was held to the horse's back, sitting almost as if living, riddled, and mangled, and torn with balls. General Cleburne's mare had her fore feet on top of the works, dead in that position. General Cleburne's body was pierced with forty-nine bullets, through and through. General Strahl's horse lay by the roadside and the general by his side, both dead, and all his staff. General Gist, a noble and brave cavalier from South Carolina, was lying with his sword reaching across the breastworks still grasped in his hand. He was lying there dead. All dead! . . . The private soldier sleeps where he fell, piled in one mighty heap. . . . I cannot tell the number of others killed and wounded. God alone knows that. We'll all find out on the morning of the final resurrection.

rank-and-file soldier in the Army of Tennessee could sense imminent danger, and the situation at hand was one that alarmed them. James H. McNeilly, a chaplain in General William A. Quarles's all-Tennessee brigade, later recalled that as soon as orders were given to attack:

> The men seemed to realize that our charge on the enemy's works would be attended with heavy slaughter, and several of them came to me bringing watches, jewelry, letters, and photographs, asking me to take charge of them and send them to their families if they were killed. I had to decline, as I was going with them and would be exposed to the same danger.

In decided contrast to the many Confederates who feared the worst possible conclusion to the upcoming battle, a few Union leaders smelled victory when they learned that the fight was on. One of them, upon observing row after row of rapidly approaching Rebels, remarked that " . . . in a few brief moments . . . all that orderly grandeur would be changed to bleeding, writhing confusion, and . . . thousands of those valorous men of the South, with their chivalric officers, would pour out their life's blood. . . ."

At 4:00 P.M. first contact was made between the gallant men of Hood's Army of Tennessee and the well-entrenched soldiers of Schofield's Fourth and Twenty-third Corps. The day had been unusually warm and bright, a far cry from the weather conditions of two weeks earlier, and the early evening promised to be mild as well. Some nineteen thousand Confederate infantrymen had started the long march toward Franklin from the hills south of town. Hood refused to wait for General S. D. Lee's corps, consisting of three more divisions still on the way from Spring Hill, nor would he delay the attack while his artillery emplaced itself to provide covering fire.

While the endless lines of Southerners approached the village, Union General George D. Wagner ordered two of his three brigades to position themselves on the open ground outside the Yankee defenses at a point that left them totally unprotected to the advance of Hood's infantry. Captain John K. Shellenberger of the Sixty-fourth Ohio Infantry echoed the sentiments of many of his comrades when he wrote later that, "The opinion was . . . universal that a big blunder was being committed in forcing us to fight with our flank fully exposed in the midst of a wide field, while in plain sight in our rear was a good line of breastworks with its flank protected by the river." Shellenberger, as were all company commanders, was ordered to "hold the position to the last man, and to have my sergeants fix bayonets and to instruct my company that any man, not wounded, who should attempt to leave the line without orders, would be shot or bayonetted by the sergeants."

In the meantime, Wagner's remaining brigade—which was commanded by Colonel Emerson Opdycke and which had brought up the rear of the division—

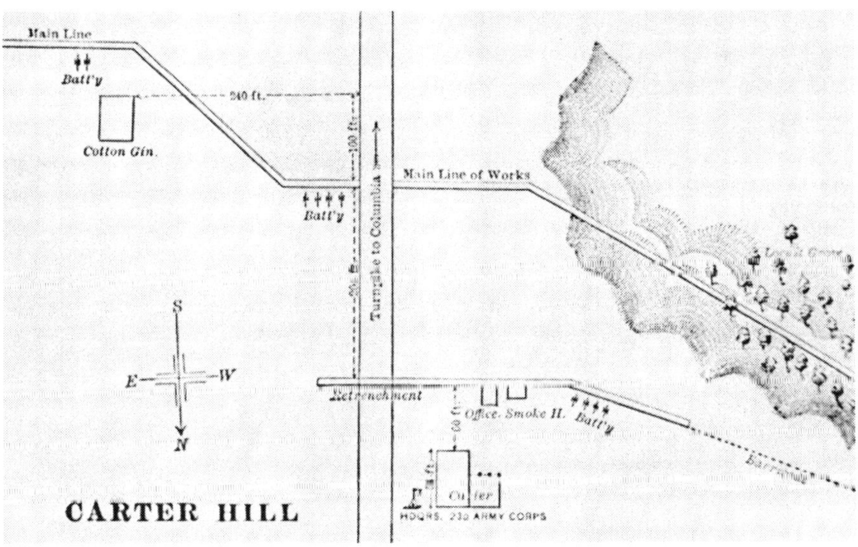

ABOVE
Much of the heaviest fighting at Franklin took place near the Carter House, where Schofield's soldiers had dug emplacements in anticipation of Hood's attack. This map was drawn by Lieutenant Colonel Moscow Carter, the brother of Tod Carter, who was killed near the family home. (Map from Cox's Battle of Franklin*)*

was ordered to take its place alongside the other two units. Opdycke refused to subject his men to such danger, and, instead marched them through the breastworks to a resting area near the Carter House. As affairs later proved, the colonel's disobedience of orders saved much of the Union army from annihilation at Franklin.

"It was the grandest sight I ever beheld," Lieutenant Edwin H. Rennolds of the Fifth Tennessee Regiment exclaimed, as thousands of his fellow infantrymen poured across the open ground that lay between Winstead Hill and the Union breastworks near the Carter House to attack the soldiers of General Wagner's two exposed brigades. Within minutes, Union troops were falling back, attempting feverishly to reach the protection of the earthworks that lay several score yards behind them. On and on came the Confederate attackers, each one screaming and yelling at the top of his lungs, while the bands continued to blare out their martial music. "Wagner's men broke in confusion. . . . The men fought like demons," wrote Captain Irving Buck, an adjutant on General Pat Cleburne's staff, adding that, "Often the combatants were near enough to use clubbed muskets and the bayonet."

At about the time it appeared that the Confederates would rout Schofield's defenders, the men of Opdycke's brigade, now rested and ready for a fight, rushed into the melee. Gradually, Opdycke's men pushed the gray-clad soldiers back and closed the gap in the earthworks. The battle continued into the night, and during the exchange, horrified troopers on both sides watched helplessly as the lifeblood of their companions drained into the cotton fields of the Carter plantation. One of those severely wounded during the action was Major Arthur MacArthur, the nineteen-year-old commander of the Twenty-fourth Wisconsin Infantry Regiment who later became the highest-ranking officer in the United States Army and the father of General Douglas MacArthur.

The sights and sounds on the battlefield were horrifying. A colonel in the Sixty-fourth Ohio Infantry Regiment recalled later that:

> I saw a Confederate soldier, close to me, thrust one of our men through with the bayonet, and before he could draw his weapon from the . . . wound his brains were scattered on all of us that stood near, by the butt of a musket swung with terrific force by some big fellow whom I could not recognize in the grim dirt and smoke that enveloped us. And as I glanced hurriedly around and heard the dull thuds, I turned from the sickening sight and was glad to hide the vision in work with a hatchet, for I had broken my sword.

Before the gunfire ceased around 10:00 P.M., the soldiers of the Army of Tennessee had charged Schofield's defenders more than a dozen times, only to

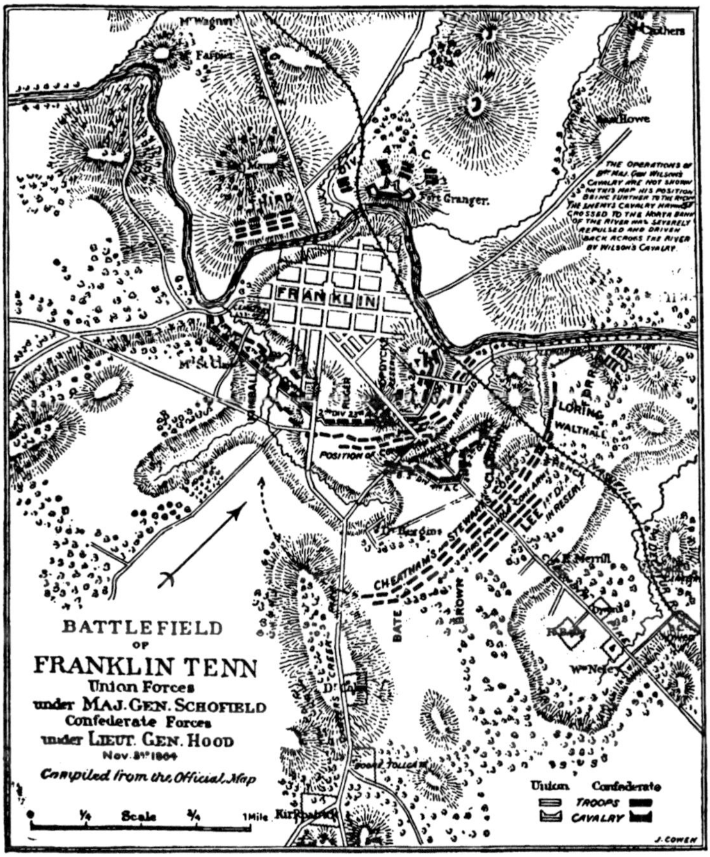

ABOVE
Map of the Franklin battlefield, showing deployment of Confederate and Union forces on November 30, 1864. (Map from Century Magazine*)*

be hurled back each time. Among those killed outright in the intense action were five Confederate generals: Patrick R. Cleburne, John Adams, States Rights Gist, Hiram B. Granbury, and Otho F. Strahl. Another general officer, John C. Carter, was mortally wounded and died several days later. Eight other Southern generals were wounded and one was captured.

Sergeant Major S. A. Cunningham left a penetrating recollection of the final moments in the life of one of the slain Confederate generals, Otho Strahl, as well as a vivid description of the intense fighting that took place near the Carter House and the Carter cotton gin, located on the opposite side of the Columbia

Pike. Eyewitness accounts of the deaths of the other generals are equally as moving. Years later, Cunningham wrote that:

> I was near General Strahl, who stood in the ditch and handed up guns to those posted to fire them. I had passed to him my short Enfield (noted in the regiment) about the sixth time. The man who had been firing, cocked it and was taking deliberate aim, when he was shot and tumbled down dead into the ditch upon those killed before him. When the men so exposed were shot down, their places were supplied by volunteers until these were exhausted, and it was necessary for General Strahl to call for others. He turned to me, and though I was several feet back from the ditch, I rose up immediately, and walking over the wounded and dead, took position with one foot upon the pile of bodies of my dead fellows, and the other upon the embankment, and fired guns which the General himself handed up to me until he, too, was shot down. One other man had position on my right, and assisted in the firing.
>
> The battle lasted until not an efficient man was left between us and the Columbia Pike, some fifty yards to our right, and hardly any behind us to hand up guns. Indeed but few of us were then left alive. It seemed as if we had no choice but to surrender or try to get away. When I asked General Strahl for counsel, he simply answered, "Keep firing." But just as the man to my right was shot, and fell against me with terrible groans, the General too was shot. He threw up his hands, falling on his face, and I thought him dead, but in asking the dying man, who still lay against my shoulders as he sank forever, how he was wounded, the General, who had not been killed, thinking my question was to him, raised up saying that he was shot in the neck, and called for Colonel Stafford to turn over his command. He crawled over the dead, the ditch being three deep, about twenty feet to where Colonel Stafford was. Staff officers and others started to carry him to the rear, but he received another shot, and directly the third, which killed him instantly. Colonel Stafford was dead in the pile, as the morning light disclosed, with his feet wedged in at the bottom, other dead across and under him after he fell; leaving his body half standing as if ready to give command to the dead!

In other parts of the corpse-strewn battlefield at Franklin, came tales of pathos and tragedy that would rival a Greek play. One story relates that:

> The dead, cold and stiff bodies were laying in every conceivable posture, all with ghastly faces and glassy eyes. . . . At the gap in the works where the pike road went through . . . were lying a Confederate and a Federal soldier, both with bayonets sent through their bodies. It was plain to see that they were each other's victims;

> they both had hands on their guns. Close by a Georgia colonel and a Federal major lay, their positions indicating that they had slain each other with pistols. . . .

Elsewhere, other dramas were being played out. During the action near the Carter gin house, in which Opdycke's Brigade plugged the hole in the Union breastworks created by the men of Cheatham's corps, a member of the 88th Illinois Infantry Regiment was seen giving a badly wounded Southern colonel in the Missouri Infantry a drink of water from his own canteen and attempting to extract the colonel's mangled body from the heap of dying and wounded men that surrounded it.

☆ ☆ ☆

While history was being made on the plains south of Franklin, an equally dramatic and moving scene involving one of the town's native sons was being played out closeby. When young Theodorick (Tod) Carter left his home on the outskirts of Franklin in 1861 to fight in the War, he could not have realized that the next time he saw his family would be from his deathbed. Marching off to a hero's departure, Tod believed, like most other Southerners, that the ensuing conflict would be a short-lived one and that he would be back home with his family in no time at all.

ABOVE
The Carter House as it appeared several years after the war. Very likely, it looked much the same during the bloody Battle of Franklin. (Photograph from Scofield's Retreat from Pulaski*)*

EYEWITNESS TO THE BATTLE OF FRANKLIN: A WOMAN'S VIEW

The soldiers were not the only ones to suffer during the Battle of Franklin. Many of the women and girls of the town spent untold numbers of hours volunteering their services as nurses to see after the wounded and dying of both armies. Frances (Fannie) Courtney, a nineteen-year-old woman who lived with her family—split in its loyalties toward the North and the South—was one of these. The following letter, written in March 1865, describes some of Fannie's recollections of the heat of battle.

I hasten to give you an account of the Battle of Franklin, together with a statement of the facts concerning the hospitals and the wounded during the stay of the Rebels, a period of seventeen days, after the Battle. The details of the memorable engagement of November 30th will, of course, be according to my opportunity for personal observation, while terror stirred my soul. The other facts transpired in calmer moments, when my heart was filled with a holy sense of duty toward the suffering.

On the morning of the 30th of November the retreating army arrived at this place, tired and many almost exhausted. But, notwithstanding this, they commenced immediately throwing up breastworks. You would have been astonished to see how quick the work was completed, and with what strength. We felt great uneasiness of mind, fearing that there would be a great battle. We asked of almost everyone passing if that would be the case. They replied "We will only skirmish with the Rebels till we get our wagon trains away, and then we will invite them to Nashville."

But we were doomed to disappointment; about half past three o'clock I was sitting at the dinner table, when I heard the roar of artillery. I ran into the yard to listen. There was a skirmishing for a few minutes only, when, with a tremendous yell, the Rebels made a charge along the whole line. The bullets were falling so thick it was unsafe to remain longer. I stood within the door, and in a few minutes all was in perfect confusion. Men, women, and children were running in every direction, together with unmanageable teams, loose horses and mules. My position was no longer safe. I hastened to the cellar with the rest of my family and neighbors who sought protection with us. But alas! The charges were fearful, and made with redoubled fury the darker it grew.

About 10 o'clock suddenly the firing ceased for a few minutes. I heard persons in the sitting room above. It proved to be some Federal officers off duty for a time, who stopped to let us know how the Battle was going. All the evening other portions of the house and the entire front yard were filled with soldiers who were almost worn out with the hard marches of the last few days, and the tough work of the morning. . . . Another desperate charge! Such yells! I can never forget them. I ran again to the cellar. In a very short time three wounded Federal soldiers came in from the battlefield, and stopped in the yard, for they could go no farther. I called to the men outside to bring them into the cellar. Two were slightly wounded. The third was struck in the arm, and the main artery was cut. He was bleeding profusely. One of the neighbors ran up at the risk of his life and brought a bucket of water. My mother had some cotton near. I poured water on the wound for some time. I then put cotton on each side where the ball entered and came out, bound it up with my handkerchief, and with two others belonging to my sister and little brother, made for him a sling. He lay down to rest, but complained of being cold from loss of blood. I had nothing to cover him with. What was I to do? A thought struck me. I took off my woolen skirt and tucked it around him. He remained for some time, though all the while bleeding a little. His comrades decided to try to overtake an ambulance with him, and I suppose they did, as they did not return.

Soon a fire broke out in town. It was fearful enough, for we thought of nothing else but being burned alive in the cellar, as there was no way of getting out if the fire continued to spread. The Rebels could see the position of our forces, and consequently, the fighting was more terrible. Several buildings were consumed, but thanks to a kind Providence, the fire was extinguished by the timely interference of soldiers, assisted by citizens. About thirteen charges in all were made by the Rebels.

At midnight the Federal Army began to retreat, the wagon trains being safe, and gradually the firing ceased. Oh! how grateful to God we felt that it was over, as we thought of the dying and the dead on the battlefield. Then we emerged from our place of refuge. I dragged beds into my mother's room for us to rest there, as we wished to spend the remainder of the night of terror together. I could not sleep, for I longed to go to the battlefield to alleviate suffering, and, at least, do all in my power to make the wounded more comfortable until they could be brought to hospitals.

At 3 o'clock, again, such cannonading! What could it mean? It shook the earth, the house; everything seemed in motion above and below. It was a farewell salute sent by the rebels to the retreating army, now far away. I was so frightened I sprang up and aroused everyone to get to the cellar immediately or we should be killed. I remained close to the house, to do which, though it took me not more than two minutes, seemed an age. Just as I reached the cellar door a shell exploded close by, and had I been three seconds later in passing, I should have been struck by some of the fragments which flew about. How grateful we felt to God that we were spared! But amidst our joy we thought of the dead ones who had fallen to find graves in a strange land, and of the suffering ones lying exposed on the field; of the desolate homes, and the many hearts stricken with sorrow when the sad tidings should reach them.

While we were talking and thinking about the dreadful night we had passed, we heard footsteps at the door. The bell rang, and as with strange, nervous feelings I opened the door, who should stand, face to face with me but my own dear brother and cousin? They were just from the field. Words are inadequate to express my happiness. They had been in the Rebel army over three years. We had not seen them for two years. There was consternation in the house for awhile. My mother was overjoyed that she was once more permitted to clasp her boy to her heart. He remained with us one day and night, and then joined his command near Murfreesboro.

During the past three years, Carter had fought valiantly in several campaigns with the Army of Tennessee under a number of commanders. Never once in that period had he been furloughed home to see his family. As a captain in John Bell Hood's advancing army, he now anxiously looked upon his beloved village, not as the innocent youngster who had left in a shower of hurrahs and band music, but as a seasoned veteran who wanted nothing more than for the awful bloodletting to be over.

During the late evening of November 30, while the noise of small arms fire still echoed across the Columbia Pike, the Carter family was holed up in the basement of the farm house for protection. Moscow Carter, Tod's older brother who was home on parole from Union captivity, later recalled that, "Bullets rained against the house, and a cannon ball went crashing though." The following day, after the fighting had stopped, hundreds of bullet holes were counted in the south wall of the Carter plantation office that stood only a few feet away from the house.

A messenger hastily rode up and knocked on the door of the Carter home and informed Tod's frightened relatives that their kinsman had been severely wounded just a few feet away in his own backyard. The battered youth was carefully delivered to his parents' waiting arms. Eight-year-old Alice McPhail Nichol, who lived with the Carter family, remembered that Tod had been found "lying face down thrown over his horse's head." He had been shot nine times in both arms, both legs, and in the head. Tod died two days later, finally at home after being separated from his family for so long, and was laid to rest about a mile north of the home place, in Franklin's Rest Haven Cemetery.

Elsewhere in Franklin, civilians were hurrying frantically about trying to keep out of the line of fire and attempting to render first aid to the casualties on both sides. Practically all available business buildings and churches in town, as well as many private residences, were used as field hospitals. Forty-one of the hospitals were used for the Confederate wounded and three were reserved for Union soldiers.

ABOVE
The loss to the Confederacy of Irish-born Major-General Patrick R. Cleburne at Franklin was second only to that of Stonewall Jackson. (Photograph courtesy of the Carter House)

Frances Courtney was a nineteen-year-old girl who lived with her parents on present-day Church Street in a house that still stands. Despite the fact that her own brother was in General Nathan Bedford Forrest's cavalry, Frances, as well as her mother, was a Northern sympathizer. She and her mother spent considerable time during the evening and night of November 30, and well into the morning of December 1, ministering to Union soldiers in their own home and others in the area. "All the evening other portions of the house and the entire front yard were filled with soldiers who were almost worn out with the hard marches of the last few days, and the tough work of the morning," she wrote later. Continuing, she tells of an occasion when she:

> heard an awful groan; someone had been struck in the back yard. I went to the door, and within a few yards of me lay a Federal soldier who, I supposed, had been wounded a short time before the firing ceased. I sent one of the soldiers out to look after his comrade and to give him water. But he did not have to remain long; the wound proved to be mortal, and the poor man expired.

☆ ☆ ☆

At 7:10 P.M. on November 30, General Schofield dispatched a message to General Thomas at Nashville advising his superior of the activities in Franklin for the past few hours. "The enemy made a heavy and persistent attack with about two corps, commencing at 4 P.M.and lasting until after dark," telegraphed

Schofield, adding that Hood's army was "repulsed at all points, with very heavy loss. . . ." Within a matter of minutes, Thomas replied, "Your telegram is just received. It is glorious news, and I congratulate you and the brave men of your command. . . ."

At around midnight, Schofield ordered his army to head north to Nashville and the protection of General Thomas's huge Union garrison, leaving Hood and his commanders at Franklin wondering what to do next. The Battle of Franklin was over. As the old saying goes, the rest is history. Neither side was a clear winner. Schofield could not claim victory when he retreated the same day he arrived from a position he had been requested to hold for three days. Nor, could Hood boast victorious, since success for him would have meant the annihilation of Schofield's command, which instead survived to fight another day.

In terms of lives lost, Franklin was indeed one of the bloodiest battles of the entire War. Confederate casualties numbered around seventy-three hundred, while the Union army suffered more than twenty-five hundred. The town was severely damaged, and fear and deprivation were everywhere. "Bloody Franklin," as the battle has often been called, truly plunged its sleepy namesake and the entire countryside roundabout into a state of depression, both economic and psychological, from which it took years to recover.

But, there was still more to come. Residents of Frankin had not seen the last of John Bell Hood, nor of the Army of Tennessee. Little did they know when December 1 dawned that in a little over two weeks, the remnants of the ragtag Confederate Army would once more march through town, only this time, in retreat from its defeat at Nashville.

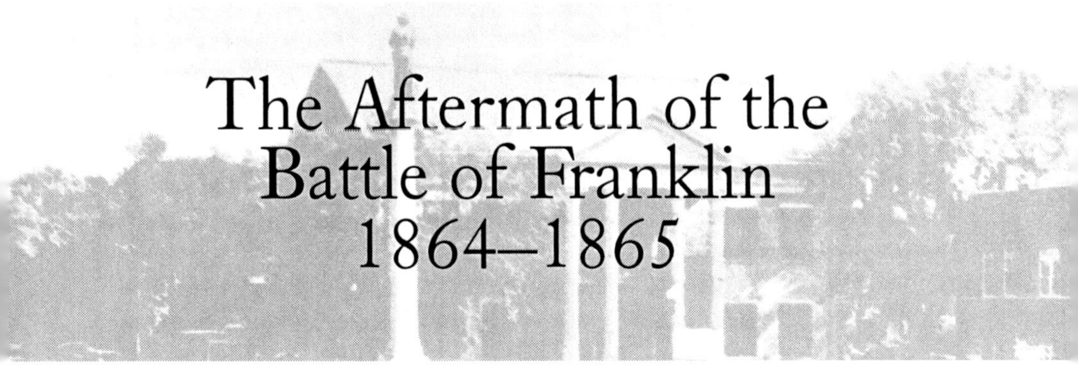

The Aftermath of the Battle of Franklin 1864–1865

ON DECEMBER 1, 1864, with the sun rising slowly in the east, General John Bell Hood shook his head in disbelief as he stared at the fresh wagon tracks in the muddy banks of the Harpeth River. For the second time in as many days, the enemy Union forces led by Hood's old West Point friend and classmate, General John M. Schofield, had slipped past him and were now on their way to help fortify General George Thomas's command at Nashville.

Within hours after Schofield's departure from the Franklin battlefield during the wee hours of the morning, Hood and his Army of Tennessee crossed the Harpeth River and marched north. When he approached Nashville, he knew that he could either gather his forces and lay a partial "siege" to the city, or he could bypass the capital and leave General Thomas's vastly superior forces to his rear. Obviously, there was no real choice, and General Hood began to formulate his battle plan.

The next day saw General Hood and his commanders establishing their positions on the outer edges of Nashville, and elements of his army conducted a few operations against the Federal blockhouses in the area. In the meantime, General Thomas, the commander of occupied Nashville, received instructions from the War Department in Washington to attack Hood's army at once. Thomas, however, was not satisfied that his troops were quite up to the fight, so he deferred risking a major defeat by not making contact with Hood's advance elements.

In an attempt to create a diversion and to recapture as much Middle Tennessee ground as possible, General Hood, on December 5, ordered General

Nathan Bedford Forrest to strike at the Federal garrison at Murfreesboro and to occupy the small town on the Stone's River. Forrest hit the Rutherford County village like lightning, but the Union forces there were too well entrenched and too strong from many months of occupation to buckle. Forrest came up empty-handed.

The leadership of the Union Army, by this time, was getting paranoid over the situation at Nashville, and General Ulysses Grant, on the sixth of the month, was explicit in his orders to Thomas. "Attack Hood at once . . .," he demanded, adding, "There is great danger of delay. . . ." Still, the hardheaded Thomas thought he knew the situation better than either his commander, Grant, or the politicians in Washington, and once again, he restrained from making the attack. By the next day, in the absence of positive information from Nashville, the War Department was in a furor over Thomas's insubordination. General Grant even suggested to the U.S. secretary of war that the stubborn Thomas should be replaced with a commander who would follow orders.

On December 8, 1864, General Thomas telegraphed the War Department that he could not possibly assault Hood's army before the eleventh. Fate must have been on his side, because when dawn cracked on December 9, it was accompanied by freezing rain. The rain and intense cold weather continued on into the next day, and neither man nor beast had any business being outside if it could be helped. Hearing nothing but bad news, the Federal authorities were frantic. On the thirteenth, General Grant ordered General John Logan to go to Nashville immediately and to relieve General Thomas of his command if Thomas had not attacked General Hood by the time he got there.

Meanwhile, the sleet had stopped, and although it was still unbearably cold, the weather appeared to moderate somewhat. Accordingly, General Thomas advised Washington on December 14, that the ice had melted, and that if the weather continued to clear, he would launch a major assault on the Army of Tennessee the next day.

True to his word, early on the morning of December 15, 1864, General Thomas and his Army of the Cumberland roared out of the protection of the ring of Federal forts which partially surrounded Nashville and closed ranks with Hood's Army of Tennessee. Hood had positioned his command in a perimeter four miles long, reaching from a point between the Murfreesboro and Nolensville Roads, through the present-day neighborhood around Thompson Lane and Franklin Road, to Hillsboro Road in today's Green Hills vicinity. An infantry brigade near the Belle Meade Mansion on the Harding Road and a small contingent of cavalry, which posted itself between the Charlotte Road and the Cumberland River, rounded out Hood's entire thirty-thousand-man force.

Tired, sick, ill-clothed, and bitterly cold, the brave Confederates faced close to fifty-five thousand well-fed, adequately equipped Union troops, all of whom, except Schofield's reinforcements from Franklin, had been sitting out the last few months of the War in the warm, protected, and well-supplied camp at Nashville. The Army of Tennessee fought valiantly, and although the lines had to be withdrawn and tightened, Hood was still holding his position around the strategic Franklin Pike at nightfall. Thomas, on the other hand, claimed the day—and rightfully so—as his. When the telegraph relayed the victory message to Washington, General Grant canceled his intended trip to Nashville. President Lincoln even sent his personal congratulations to Thomas now that it was apparent that the old veteran knew what he was talking about after all.

But, the battle was not over yet, and the morning of December 16 opened with more freezing rain and snow. Union action in the Granny White Pike area and around Shy's Hill near the Hillsboro Pike breached the Southern lines left and right. From midafternoon on, the Confederates were in retreat with the Union Army hot on their trail. Hood's barefoot, cold, and hungry troops "fled in confusion," wrote General Thomas, adding that they were "hopelessly broken."

When the two-day affair was over, General Thomas's army had suffered a few over three thousand casualties, including only 387 men killed. Hood's losses, while never officially confirmed, appeared to reach well over six thousand. Some historians have since noted that, for such an extended and fierce battle, casualties on both sides were extremely low. Yet, as crippled as the Army of Tennessee was, it was still a fighting unit and was not totally destroyed as some writers have indicated.

Nashville's own late Stanley Horn, the distinguished chronicler of both the Army of Tennessee and the Battle of Nashville, has written that the conflict at the Tennessee capital city was in reality the only decisive battle fought during the entire War Between the States. Horn claims that Nashville was the "climatic engagement," and that after Hood was defeated at Nashville, "the outcome of the war was beyond question; it was then merely a matter of time."

Although Hood—in the light of hindsight—had little chance to retake Nashville, there is little doubt that he believed he could. Likewise, he had Union commanders—from General Thomas in Nashville, all the way through Ulysses S. Grant and Abraham Lincoln in Washington—worried that he might just succeed. Of course, his plan failed, and the War ended four months later. On the other hand, however, had he been successful and reoccupied Nashville and pushed on beyond the city to the Ohio River, the United States might well have sued the Confederate command for peace. In fact, General Grant, himself, all but admitted this when he remarked later that, if the War

A TALE OF NURSES

The days following the awful battle at Franklin produced many heroines, many feats of bravery and valor, and many heart-breaking acts of kindness and compassion by the ladies of Franklin. "Carnton," the plantation home of Colonel John McGavock and his wife, Caroline Winder McGavock, was used as a hospital during the battle. Situated a couple of miles from downtown, off the Lewisburg Pike, the house stood close to the main Union trenches south of town and was just about the only structure in the neighborhood that could hold large numbers of wounded.

Mrs. McGavock, mistress of "Carnton," became known as the "Good Samaritan of Williamson County" for her selfless service as a nurse and friend to the scores of wounded Confederate soldiers who found their way to her door. "In all the annals of war, filled as it is with the great and noble deeds of great and noble women, none exceed and few equal in true merit, the noble sympathy of Mrs. John McGavock," wrote Colonel W. D. Gale, in a letter back home to his wife. Continuing, Gale revealed that:

> *When day dawned we found ourselves near her house—on her lawn—which was in the rear of our line. The house is one of the large old-fashioned houses of the better class in Tennessee, two stories high, with many rooms, and every arrangement for comfort. This was taken as a hospital, and the wounded, in hundreds, were brought to it during the Battle, and all the night after. Every room was filled, every bed had two poor, bleeding fellows, every spare space, niche, and corner under the stairs, in the hall, everywhere—but one room for her own family. And when the noble old house could hold no more, the yard was appropriated until the wounded and the dead filled that, and all were not yet provided for. Our doctors were deficient in bandages, and she began by giving her old linen, then her towels and napkins, then her sheets and tablecloths, then her husband's shirts and her own undergarments.*
>
> *During all this time the surgeons plied their dreadful work amid the sighs and moans and death rattle. Yet, amid it all, this noble woman, the very impersonation of divine sympathy and tender pity, was active and constantly at work. During the night neither she nor any of the household slept, but dispensed tea and coffee and such stimulants as she had, and that, too, with her own hands. Unaffrighted by the sight of blood, unawed by horrid wounds, unblanched by ghastly death, she walked from room to room, from man to man, her very skirts stained in blood, the incarnation of pity and mercy. Is it strange that all who were there praise and call her blessed?*

Francis Courtney also ministered to the wounded, but she chose to nurse the Union victims of the conflict. Continuing the letter in which Fannie gave her recollections of the battle, here she shares some of the hair-raising experiences that she and her family endured in the days following November 30, 1864.

Early the next morning after the Battle I went to the field. The sight was dreadful. It seemed that I could scarcely move for fear of stepping on men either dead or wounded. Some were cold and stiff, others with the lifeblood ebbing out, unconscious of all around, while others were writhing in agony, calling, "Water! Water!"; I can hear them even now.

The hardest fighting was done near the cotton gin, not far from the pike leading to Columbia, and near the locust grove where the gallant 72nd Illinois stood. It was near the gin that the Rebel General Cleburne fell, and also General Adams, whose horse still lies across the breastworks. Six of the Rebel generals were killed. I could not look upon such sights long, but hurried back to care for the wounded. There were forty-four hospitals in town three for the Federal wounded and the rest for the Confederates. Red flags were waving from unoccupied dwellings, the seminaries, churches, and every business house in town.

My mother and I took charge of a hundred and twenty wounded men, who occupied the Presbyterian Church, it being the largest Federal hospital, and with what we could spare assisted at another which was in a house owned by my mother and near our own home. When we first went to the hospital the wounded men told us they had had nothing to eat for two days. We first furnished them with bread, meat, tea, and coffee, every little luxury we could prepare, for several days. Then they drew scanty rations from the Rebels, flour the color of ashes and a little poor beef not suitable for well men, much less for wounded. All the cooking was done, and in truth, everything eatable furnished, at our house.

We fed the men twice a day. Sometimes at 10 o'clock at night we would carry them something prepared with our own hands. Many had been robbed not only of their blankets and overcoats but of their coats, and were lying on the floor upon handfuls of straw, with nothing else to protect or cover them. We furnished them all the bedding we could spare, and made cotton pillows for all. There were no bandages to be had, and I made what I could out of my own underclothing. We would get up at daylight and with the help of servants commence cooking their breakfast. We never had time to rest, only as we sat down to eat something hurriedly, for as soon as we had finished feeding our patients in the morning, we had to return home to prepare the next meal.

I had a sister who was very ill at the time, and we were obliged to leave her to the care of a little servant about seven years old. She said she could get along better than the poor wounded could, if we neglected them to stay with her. When my mother and I entered the hospital, how the dim eyes would brighten! The men would call out, "Oh! Mother, come this way," or "Fanny, please come here, I'm so glad to see you, I know you will do something for me." The exclamation of all was, "Oh! dear, I do not know what we should do if it were not for you and your mother. We should have starved."

I must not forget to tell you of my little brother, twelve years old, who always went with us to the hospital and would raise the weary heads of the soldiers to give them coffee or water, and feed those who were not able to feed themselves. He even went upon the battlefield and worked hard, covering the dead who were not half buried. . . .

had continued into mid-1865, the secession of the South would have been conceded by the Federal government in Washington.

So, General Hood's dream of a northern invasion on the far side of the Ohio River ended on December 16, 1864, at Nashville. Now, the tired and haggard commander had something more immediate that he had to take care of. Somehow, he must get the crippled Army of Tennessee to relative safety in Mississippi. To accomplish this, he knew of only one avenue of march, and that was back through Franklin.

☆ ☆ ☆

The day following the grand finale for Hood's disheveled army at Nashville, the United States secretary of war, Edwin M. Stanton, telegraphed General Ulysses S. Grant at his headquarters in New Jersey. "Thomas victorious yesterday. Hood's army broken; driven back to the Brentwood Hills; many prisoners and cannon taken; pursuit to be renewed to-day." Less than ten hours later, the proud and victorious Thomas, himself, advised Grant that:

> We have pressed the enemy to-day beyond Franklin, capturing his hospitals, containing over 1,500 wounded and about 150 of our wounded. In addition to the above, General Knipe [Joseph Farmer] commanding a division of cavalry, drove the enemy's rear guard through Franklin to-day, capturing about 250 prisoners and 5 battle-flags, with very little loss on our side. Citizens of Franklin represent Hood's army as completely demoralized. . . .

The Army of Tennessee's retreat from Nashville was disastrous. Artillery was left on the field, weapons were tossed aside, and men and animals struggled against a combination of hunger, cold, and Union rear-guard harassment. General Hood's new mission became the task of getting his ragtag army as far south as he could in as little time as possible, while sacrificing a minimum of the remaining men. In addition to the human enemy, the weather even plotted against Hood. A new winter storm promised to cause much misery among the ill-clothed and poorly fed Confederate ranks.

By 8:00 P.M. on December 17, Schofield's old Fourth Army Corps which had earlier fought so fiercely at Franklin and now under the command of General Thomas J. Wood, had reestablished its headquarters in the town. At this point, the rapidly retreating Hood had only one strategic factor in his favor. Despite the guerrilla tactics of the Union troops against the Confederate rear-guard fleeing Nashville, most of the Army of Tennessee had been able to get through Franklin by 10:30 A.M. on the seventeenth, well before the Yankees could secure the crossing of the Harpeth River. The Union pursuit was extremely slow due to the engineers' inability to repair or rebuild the bridge "owing to the rapid rise in the river, the swiftness of the current, and the amount of driftwood coming down the stream."

ABOVE
Most of General Hood's ragtag Army of Tennessee retreated through Franklin on December 17, 1864, on its way to Tupelo, Mississippi. Hood resigned his command one month later, but the Army went on to fight again in North Carolina, before finally surrendering on April 26, 1865. (Drawing from Battles and Leaders of the Civil War*)*

But, the Union general staff and cavalry had succeeded in fording the Harpeth and establishing themselves on the south side of the stream, while the majority of the army was stranded along the north bank. The cavalry, therefore, was able to pester the retreating Confederate army out of Franklin. Near Thompson's Station, according to a Union dispatch, "a division of infantry, a brigade of cavalry, and . . . three guns" were captured. Meanwhile, back in Franklin, tensions ran high as plans materialized to move the remainder of the troops and equipment across the river as soon as a bridge was completed, or when pontoons arrived from Nashville, whichever came first. For the time being, Union intelligence reports continued to flood the telegraph lines with such information as "The rebel army is in full retreat down the Columbia Pike," "The rebels are on a great skedaddle . . .," and ". . . never saw a worse rabble; they are completely demoralized."

In his memoirs, Private Sam Watkins, from neighboring Maury County, confirmed that his beloved Army of Tennessee was, indeed, on the run. Years after the affair, he wrote:

> Hood's whole army was routed and in full retreat. Wagon trains, cannon, artillery, cavalry, and infantry were all blended in inextricable confusion. Broken down and jaded horses and mules refused to pull, and the badly-scared drivers looked like their eyes would pop out of their heads from fright. Wagon wheels, interlocking each other, soon clogged the road, and wagons, horses, and provisions were left indiscriminately. . . . General Frank Cheatham and General Loring tried to form a line at Brentwood, but the line they formed was like trying to stop the current of Duck river with a fish net. . . . I saw a wagon and team abandoned, and I unhitched one of the horses and rode on horse-back to Franklin, where a surgeon tied up my broken finger, and bandaged up my bleeding thigh. My boot was full of blood, and my clothing saturated with it. I was at General Hood's headquarters. He was much agitated and affected, pulling his hair with his one hand (he had but one), and crying like his heart would break. I pitied him, poor fellow. I asked him for a wounded furlough, and he gave it to me. I never saw him afterward. . . .

December 17 brought more excitement to the Union command. Schofield telegraphed Thomas, telling him that, "citizens on the road in rear of where we fought yesterday report that the universal testimony of rebels, officers and men, is that Forrest [General Nathan Bedford Forrest] was killed . . . at Murfreesborough. . . ." The report proved to be an unfounded rumor, and the wily "Wizard of the Saddle" continued to render valorous service to the retreating Confederates by taking up a position at the rear of Hood's southward-retreating column and protecting it from the hit-and-run tactics of Union General James Wilson's cavalry.

For the next few days, Union engineers continued work on the Harpeth River bridge, as well as the railroad linking Nashville to Franklin, Columbia, and points south. Having received little recent intelligence from Middle Tennessee, the U.S. army's chief of staff, General H. W. Halleck, wired General Thomas from Washington on December 21, reiterating "the vast importance of a hot pursuit of Hood's army." Thomas promptly replied that:

> General Hood's army is being pursued as rapidly and as vigorously as it is possible for one army to pursue another. We cannot control the elements. . . . I . . . have been enabled to drive the enemy beyond Duck River, crossing two streams with my troops, and driving the enemy from position to position, without the aid of pontoons, and with but little transportation to bring up supplies of provisions and ammunition. I am doing all in my power to crush Hood's army, and, if it be possible, will destroy it; but pursuing an enemy through an exhausted country, over mud roads, completely sogged with heavy rains, is no child's play, and cannot be accomplished as quickly as thought of.

At about the same time Thomas telegraphed Halleck, his headquarters "in the field" received a transmittal from Franklin which related that, "There is no probability of the railroad bridge being done to-day." Accordingly, the men charged with repairing or replacing the turnpike bridge were pulled off to help with the railroad trestle, which was being delayed because of the inability to clear the debris of the old bridge out of the Harpeth. Later in the day, however, the railroad bridge was finally repaired and the lieutenant colonel in charge of the engineers happily wired Thomas's headquarters that, "Construction train is across the Harpeth. I leave for Spring Hill. . . ."

☆ ☆ ☆

While the armies of Hood and Thomas prepared for battle at Nashville during mid-December 1864, the civilian population of Franklin was striving to make ends meet, while at the same time taking care of both the Confederate and Union wounded. To make bad matters worse, the weather, which had been warm and balmy on the day of the big battle, suddenly turned ugly, and freezing rains and temperatures hung around for days. Hardin Figuers, a youngster who lived in Franklin at the time, later gave a vivid description of conditions in the little town on the Harpeth during the early days of December. He wrote:

> The rain on the third day after the battle turned into a snow, and during the eighteen days that the Confederates occupied the town it was the most terrible spell of weather I ever knew. There were snow, sleet, and ice continually, with the thermometer down to zero.
>
> Food got scarcer and scarcer each day. Many a day I went out through the country in an old dump cart hunting for food. We would take a large wash kettle, holding about twenty gallons, and make it full of soup and plenty of red pepper. For this soup I brought in from the country Irish potatoes, cabbage, dried beans, and turnips, and in making it we used any kind of meat obtainable. The soldiers thought this was great diet: in fact, the best they had had for more than a year.

Soon after the battle, attempts had been made to bury the dead, but the job became one of monumental proportions. Near the Carter House, where some of the most intense fighting occurred, Confederate funeral details collected and buried corpses on both sides of the Columbia Pike. The teenager, Hardin Figuers, reported that some of the Union dead were not interred for three days after the battle and then were "buried generally just as they had fallen by pulling dirt from the breastworks down on them." A sudden rainfall during the mass burial of these Union troopers so saturated the decaying bodies that "the water was literally running blood."

On his way in pursuit of Hood's army after its rout at Nashville, an Ohio soldier stopped off at a hospital in Franklin to see if he could find any of his wounded friends. It was not a pretty sight. "As I stepped into the room I detected, at once, a sickening, poisonous atmosphere that seemed to suffocate me," he wrote. Continuing, he reported that:

> I supposed I could soon overcome this, and pressed on; but by the time I had gotten ten feet into the room I found that I had none too much time left if I would get out before fainting. I hurried out without getting a chance to speak to any one or anyone speaking to me. The stench arising from the putrifying wounds was really unbearable.

The same soldier then took a tour of the battlefield, which, with the exception of the removal of the human bodies, looked much the same as it did on the morning of December 1. As far as he could see, the soldier saw row after row of graves, denoting the resting places of his fallen comrades. He noted that the thousands of bullets that had raked the area on the day of the battle had so torn up the branches of nearby trees and shrubbery that "it gave the appearance of being strewn over with cotton." And, sadly, he reported that the "putrifying carcass" of Confederate General John Adams's "noble horse" still lay where it had fallen almost three weeks earlier.

☆ ☆ ☆

Hindsight is a wonderful thing. It is so easy to proclaim, decades after an event occurred, that this or that should have been done instead of what was. The art of war seems to provide a particularly intriguing issue when it comes to gatherings of modern day arm-chair historians quick to condemn—or at least criticize—the tactics and strategies of past conflicts. The Battle of Franklin has had its share of searches for the truth, interpretations, and "what if" theories proposed by pupils of history, both amateur and professional. General Hood's prudence in making a frontal assault on Schofield's well-fortified position—especially without the support of his artillery and a large contingent of infantry—has been seriously questioned by military strategists ever since the end of the War.

It is not the purpose of this work to investigate Hood's judgment on that long ago day in November 1864. Although in his book, *Advance and Retreat*, he defended his actions both at Franklin and those of the previous night at Spring Hill, other voices, even some from the past who were present at the action, disagree. Samuel T. Foster, a thirty-five-year-old captain in the 24th Texas Cavalry Regiment, Granbury's Brigade, Cleburne's Division at Franklin, was one of these. In the journal that he kept of his wartime service as "one of Cleburne's command," Foster wrote one of the most scathing criticisms ever uttered about Hood by one of his own men.

> Gen. Hood has betrayed us (The Army of Tenn). This is not the kind of fighting he promised us at Tuscumbia and Florence Ala. when we started into Tenn.
>
> This was not a "fight with equal numbers and choice of the ground," by no means.
>
> And the wails and cries of widows and orphans made at Franklin Tenn Nov 30th 1864 will heat up the fires of the bottomless pit to burn the soul of Gen J B Hood for Murdering their husbands and fathers at that place that day. It can't be called anything else but cold blooded Murder.

"SKEDADDLING" THROUGH FRANKLIN

The withdrawal of the Army of Tennessee from Nashville and its passage through Franklin on the way to Mississippi during mid-and late December 1864, was anything but organized. Although a few of Hood's units kept some semblance of order, many others fell into disarray, and every man was on his own to reach safety the best way he could. James H. McNeilly was a chaplain and surgeon's assistant in the brigade commanded by General William A. Quarles, part of General Edward C. Walthall's division. His personal recollections of the southward retreat were published years later in the *Confederate Veteran*.

We reached Franklin in a disorganized condition, and I determined to try to get some clothes to replace my rags. I heard that an old friend of mine was living a few miles southwest of the town, and I started out to find him. After walking three or four miles I came to a considerable stream. It was much swollen, and there were neither bridge nor boat to help me across. I could not swim, and so my way seems barred. But my needs were urgent, and the prospect of clothes overcame my fears. I waded in. As I stepped cautiously along, the water came higher about me until it reached my armpits. I was about to give up and turn back when another step brought me into shallower water. I was soon on the other side, dripping with almost icy water. I walked fast to keep from freezing, and I soon reached my friend's house.

The welcome I received was most hearty, and the whole family set about making me comfortable. My wet clothes were removed, and I was arrayed in a shirt and pair of trousers belonging to the old gentleman, head of the household. The trousers, of black doeskin, were shiny from long wear, but they were fine compared with my ragged togging. They took my old clothes to dry and mend and gave me a good supper, and I expected to spend the night with them and have a good talk; but just as I settled down and was feeling quite comfortable we heard musketry-firing not far away, which I took to be from the Yankees in pursuit. I at once prepared to 'skedaddle'.

I concluded that I could get along very well without new clothes and that, as time was pressing, there was no need to mend my old ones. It might interfere with ventilation if they fitted too tight. So I put on my jacket, bundled up the rest of my duds, and started to go out to Spring Hill, where I hoped to catch up with our army. The night was intensely dark, and I had to guess my course without a single star to guide me. My friend directed me to a little creek or branch near by and to follow its course until I came to a main road, which led to Spring Hill. I made my way by the gurgling of the water. I was walking in a lane. For a hundred yards or more there was high rail fence on each side, probably the only piece of rail fence in the neighborhood. I heard a squad of horseman coming behind me. A bird could not have gone over that fence more lightly than I did. Fear lent me wings, but my agility came near landing me in the brook.

After beating about in the dark for a time I came in sight of numerous camp fires, but whether ours or the Yankees I could not tell. Making my way cautiously to the nearest one, I came upon a company of half a dozen men sitting around a fire on one side of a dense thicket of bushes. Whether they were Confederates or Federals was still the unsolved problem. The light was too dim to distinguish them clearly, and their voices were too indistinct for me to recognize their quality. So I got down on my hands and knees and crawled stealthily through the thicket until I came within a few feet of them, when I heard one of them say: "Well, we did give them Yankees the devil, anyhow." And he spoke of the attack on his division. I knew then that I was among friends, and I stepped out and found the men were of Walthall's Division. I made myself known to them when one of them said, "Parson, if we had known you were in there, we could have scared you badly by pretending to be Yankees and threatening to shoot into that thicket." I replied: "Yes; and if I had rushed out pretending to be a Yankee and ordered you to surrender, you would have done it or skedaddled."

He sacrificed those men to make the name of Hood famous; when if the History of it is ever written it will make him infamous.

He had near 10,000 men murdered around Atlanta trying to prove to the world that he was a greater man than Genl Johnson [*sic*]—Because Johnson said that Atlanta was untenable, and could not be held with the men he had against the men that Sherman had. And how small he must have felt when he had to leave there in the night to keep from being captured.

And now in order to recover from the merited disgrace of that transaction he brings this Army here into middle Tenn. and by making them false promises and false statements get these men killed—Put them into a fight where the Yanks have three lines of breastworks; the second or middle line being lined with artillery.

The men have a right to believe he told the truth and go forward to certain and sure destructions; but "Vengeance is mine Sayeth the Lord" and it will surely overtake him.

Elsewhere in his journal, Captain Foster continued his spirited tirade against the commander of the Army of Tennessee.

> . . . we were anxious to get into a fight with the Yanks; and even feared that the war would end and we never get to see one. Now we have seen too many of them, as is evidenced by our number present today—Then we were called feather bed soldiers—now we are war veterans; but Yankee bullets will kill one as quick as the other. . . . Hood was in command of a Brigade in Va. Now he is in command of a remnant of the Army of Tenn. after having butchered 10,000 of them around Atlanta Ga. and as many more in Tenn. at Franklin and Nashville, where he betrayed his whole Army—He might command a Brigade—and even a division but to command the Army, he is not the man. Genl Joe Johnston has more military sense in one day than Hood ever did or ever will have.
>
> He lost all the public property and heavy artillery at Atlanta when Sherman drove him out of that place—He lost all his artillery at Nashville Tenn. 110 pieces, all gone. After all these losses and now on the retreat out of Tenn. with the remnant of an Army that should be in winter quarters, recruiting and he afraid to show himself, and then call him a General, is a disgrace to those Generals in fact who are worthy to be so called.

But, the gallant Hood had defenders within his ranks as well. Private Sam Watkins, although questioning Hood's abilities to command so large a military unit as an entire army, nevertheless personally liked the man and refused to criticize him. In his book, *Co. "Aytch,"* Watkins later wrote:

> Hood was a good man, a kind man, a philanthropic man. . . . He was a poor general in the capacity of commander-in-chief. Had he been mentally qualified, his physical condition would have disqualified him. . . . As a soldier, he was brave, good, noble, and gallant, and fought with the ferociousness of the wounded tiger, and with the everlasting grit of the bull-dog; but as a General he was a failure in every particular.

☆ ☆ ☆

On Christmas Day 1864, the majority of the badly decimated, shoeless, and starved Army of Tennessee crossed the Tennessee River near Bainbridge, Alabama. Hood ordered General Forrest and his cavalry, along with two thousand infantrymen, to cover the army's rear from Pulaski, thus giving the main body of soldiers time to make their retreat across northern Alabama into Mississippi. His mission accomplished, Forrest, on December 27, crossed the

Tennessee and eventually joined the rest of the army at Tupelo.

Hood's once mighty army was only a remnant of what it had been when the ambitious, and perhaps vainglorious, general made his infamous decision to assault Schofield's army at Franklin. Now, less than one month later, the infantry stood at around fifteen thousand men, the strength of the cavalry was badly eroded, and the artillery and the transportation system were virtually nonexistent. General Thomas, confidant that Hood posed no further threat and expecting no more action from the crippled Confederates, called off the chase on December 27.

The War in Tennessee and the rest of the Western Theater was over. Hood resigned as the commander of the Army of Tennessee on January 13, 1865. In the meantime, several contingents of the Army were moved to North Carolina, where, once again under the command of General Joseph E. Johnston, they attempted to halt Union General William T. Sherman's advance northward out of South Carolina. On April 26, the same day that U.S. troops shot and killed the suspected assassin of President Abraham Lincoln, John Wilkes Booth, in a Virginia barn, General Johnston surrendered his army near Durham, North Carolina. Among those units that laid down their weapons during the next week and agreed to the articles of surrender were the "Williamson Grays" and the "Marion Rifles," both units mustered into service in Franklin in early 1861.

About the Author

JAMES A. CRUTCHFIELD is the author of more than forty books about American history. He is the recipient of several writing awards from the Tennessee American Revolutionary Bicentennial Commission, the American Association for State and Local History, Western Writers of America, and the Heritage Foundation of Franklin and Williamson County (Tennessee). His newspaper and magazine articles have appeared in both regional and national publications. Crutchfield lives in Franklin, Tennessee, with his wife, Regena, and their two cats.

Breinigsville, PA USA
12 October 2009

225570BV00002B/2/P

9 781577 364382